Read with Me!

Stress-Free Strategies for Building Language and Literacy

Shari Robertson   Helen Davig

Thinking Publications • Eau Claire, WI

© 2002 by Thinking Publications

Thinking Publications grants limited rights to individual professionals to reproduce and distribute pages that indicate duplication is permissible. Pages can be used for instruction only and must include Thinking Publications' copyright notice. All rights are reserved for pages without the permission-to-reprint notice. No part of these pages can be reproduced in any form, electronic or mechanical, including photocopy, recording, or any information storage and retrieval system, without permission in writing from the publisher.

09 08 07 06 05 04 03 02   8 7 6 5 4 3 2 1

Library of Congress Cataloging-in-Publication Data

Robertson, Shari, date.
    Read with me! : stress-free strategies for building language and literacy / Shari Robertson, Helen Davig.
      p. cm.
    Includes bibliographical references (p.).
    ISBN 1-888222-90-5 (pbk.)
    1. Reading—Parent participation—Handbooks, manuals, etc. 2. Children—Books and reading—Handbooks, manuals, etc. I. Title: Stress-free strategies for building language and literacy. II. Davig, Helen, date. III. Title.

LB1050.2 .R62 2002
372.41—dc21   2002022158

Printed in the United States of America
Cover design by Paul D. Modjeski
Illustrations by Jessica Martenson

THINKING PUBLICATIONS®
A Division of McKinley Companies, Inc.

424 Galloway Street • Eau Claire, WI 54703
715-832-2488 • Fax 715-832-9082
Email: custserv@ThinkingPublications.com
COMMUNICATION SOLUTIONS THAT CHANGE LIVES®

To the parents and children who have participated in *Read with Me!* sessions. Their newfound joy of reading together has been the inspiration for this book.

ABOUT THE AUTHORS

Shari Robertson, PhD, CCC-SLP, is an associate professor in the Department of Special Education and Clinical Services at Indiana University of Pennsylvania. She earned her doctorate from the University of Wisconsin–Madison in child language disorders and counseling in communicative disorders. Prior to that, she worked 16 years as a practicing speech-language pathologist and program support teacher for speech-language and early childhood programs in the West Bend, WI, public schools. She is particularly interested in investigating the efficacy of various intervention methods and delivery models. Her research involving intervention with late talkers earned the Editor's Award for the Journal of Speech-Language-Hearing Research (JSLHR) in the area of language in 1999.

Helen Davig, MA, is currently the director of the Learning Together Family Literacy Program in Holmen, WI. Previously she earned her degree in education from Viterbo University, La Crosse, WI. Helen taught kindergarten for 15 years. Her experience as a kindergarten teacher created an awareness of the need for schools to collaborate with parents to develop early language skills. Helen has presented workshops on the *Read with Me!* program through the University of Wisconsin–La Crosse, at the 2002 National Center for Family Literacy conference, and at numerous state education conferences.

CONTENTS

Preface vii

Acknowledgments ix

Introduction
    Overview 3
    Target Users 3
    Goals 4
    Program Variations 4
    Background 6
    Read with Me! Strategies 10
    How to Use the Program 13
    Measuring Progress 14

Section I: Home
    Overview 17
    Goals 18
    Organization 18
    Staff Training 18
    Funding 18
    Recruitment 20
    Program Delivery 20
    Lesson Plans and Books 20
    Data Collection 21
    Session 1: Echo Reading and Paired Reading 22
    Session 2: Questioning and Predicting 29
    Session 3: Wordless Books and Reader's Theatre 37

Section II: Older Children
    Overview 63
    Goals 64
    Session 1: Older Children 65

Contents

Section III: School
- Overview...71
- Goals..72
- Organization...72
- Staff Training...72
- Funding..73
- Recruitment..73
- Program Delivery...74
- Poetry and Chapter Books.................................75
- Data Collection..76

Section IV: Speech-Language Intervention
- Overview..113
- Goals...114
- Meeting Specific Goals and Objectives...................114

Appendices
- Appendix A: Parent Literacy Training Study.............123
- Appendix B: Expanded Book Lists........................126
- Appendix C: Purchasing Information.....................161
- Appendix D: Overhead Presentation......................162
- Appendix E: Frequently Asked Questions.................170

References
....177

PREFACE

This manual is designed for use by professionals who are interested in helping children build language and literacy skills. Although reading specialists have traditionally addressed literacy development, speech-language pathologists, given their specialized training in the development of oral and written language skills, have also become increasingly involved in designing and providing intervention programs that support development in both domains. Consequently, *Read with Me! Stress-Free Strategies for Building Language and Literacy* is especially useful to professionals who work with children who have language and communication disorders.

Recent research informs us that there are strong correlations between certain isolated skills (e.g., phonological awareness) and the development of literacy. *Read with Me!* embraces an even more fundamental premise related to success in reading. That is, if children do not enjoy reading, they will very likely not want to read. Consequently, even the best possible instruction in specific skills that support reading will be less effective for children who have not learned to view reading as a pleasurable experience.

Developed, written, and tested by a speech-language pathologist and a reading specialist, *Read with Me!* is a powerful and effective tool for helping parents and educators become active participants in the development of children's most fundamental language skills—talking and reading. Adaptable for use across a wide spectrum of age and ability levels, *Read with Me!* is a joyful and educational journey that is based on the belief that through an open exchange of information, educators and families can significantly improve the early language and literacy experiences of all children.

The use of the *Read with Me!* strategies and recommended books in clinical applications with children who have communication disorders was something of a happy accident. It developed out of a grant-funded project, *Partnerships for Literacy*, undertaken by one of the authors. This project targeted two primary goals related to language and literacy. The first goal was to provide parents with meaningful information to promote the development of their children's language and literacy skills. The second goal was to provide graduate students in speech-language pathology with hands-on experience in collaborating with parents by training them as workshop facilitators. The outcomes related to these goals were robust and exciting. However, an unplanned, but welcome, benefit of training graduate students to be workshop facilitators was that they became much more aware of the their role as speech-language pathologists in the development of language in both the oral and written modes.

Preface

We have found that word-of-mouth advertising by parents who have been involved in the program is the very best recruitment tool. One of our first attempts at the program began with a very modest goal of 50 parent contacts. By the end of the third session, we had 250! We have even had parents repeat the program just because they enjoyed it so much the first time.

Each application of the *Read with Me!* program described in this manual grew out of the parent program originally developed and implemented in the School District of Holmen, WI. It has since grown both in scope and in popularity and is currently in use by educators and parents across the nation and as far away as Sydney, Australia. We predict that once you start working with the strategies and recommended books, you will find more and more applications for them across all aspects of your professional experience. Enjoy!

**Children learn to read by being read to.
They keep reading because they learn to love to read.**

ACKNOWLEDGMENTS

The authors are grateful to all the parents, children, educators, and colleagues who have participated in this program. So many have given so unselfishly of their time and talents to ensure the success of this program! Specifically, the following people are acknowledged.

Sandy Krautkramer, Julie Jacquot, Julaine Luedtke, and Steven Lefeber from the West Bend, WI, School District, who inspire those around them through their examples of excellence.

Cynthia Jacobson, Title I Coordinator for the School District of Holmen, WI, who provided the base for many of the forms found in Section III and worked diligently to collate data to demonstrate the effectiveness of the program.

La Crosse, WI, AmeriCorps volunteers Jen Bunkers, Michelle Hanson, Chris Newcomer, and Lisa Post, who helped to implement the first kindergarten program in 1995.

The speech-language pathology graduate students at Indiana University of Pennsylvania, who were enthusiastic and patient even when things got exceedingly crazy. Special thanks to Tara Altimus, Karman Creamer, Melissa Sollenberger, Denise Smith, Jaime Bantz, and Rebecca Halteman. You all made it worth the effort!

Kindergarten program facilitators Denise Donnelly and Susan Sanders, whose enthusiasm has been essential for the continued success of the Reading Together program in the School District of Holmen.

The field reviewers—Sandy Krautkramer, Pam Diebner, Kelly Mattison, and Susan Anich—who contributed their time and talents to help us make a good idea even better.

Holmen program coordinators Cynthia Jacobson and Helen Davig developed many of the forms listed in the Section III: School. The School program has been implemented successfully as the Early Intervention Title I program in the School District of Holmen since 1995 and in the district preschool since 2000 (titled "Reading Together in Kindergarten").

Introduction

Introduction

OVERVIEW

The *Read with Me! Stress-Free Strategies for Building Language and Literacy* program provides children ages 1–11 with a strong foundation for literacy by helping them develop early reading skills through quality interactions with adults. The quality interactions consist of a child and adult engaging in six reading strategies:

1. Echo reading
2. Paired reading
3. Questioning
4. Predicting
5. Wordless books
6. Reader's theatre

The strategies are implemented by parents at home, educators at school, or both. Everything necessary to either implement the strategies directly or to teach others to implement them is furnished in this manual and on the accompanying CD-ROM. *Read with Me!* provides the lessons, training tools, recommended books to implement the strategies, and pre- and post-measurement forms. The Home and School programs are best used for children younger than second grade. However, sections for expanding the use of these strategies to older students and to those with communication disorders are included.

The *Read with Me!* program targets the fundamental skills of talking and listening as a basis for the development of literacy. Children are not expected to talk if they have not been talked to. Similarly, children are not expected to read if they have never, or seldom, been read to! Additional core early reading competencies related to the development of oral language, phonological awareness, vocabulary, and critical thinking skills are also developed when *Read with Me!* is used during reading interactions. Most importantly, *Read with Me!* helps children and adults find the joy in reading together—the most fundamental of all the foundational literacy skills. From this has sprung the philosophy of the *Read with Me!* program: Children learn to read by being read to. They keep reading because they learn to love to read.

TARGET USERS

The *Read with Me!* program is designed to be used by a variety of professionals across an array of settings. Speech-language pathologists, reading specialists, early childhood educators, and classroom teachers have used the *Read with Me!* techniques and strategies successfully to address their particular needs. The various applications described in this resource can be beneficial to children as young as 12–18 months through those in sixth grade. The strategies that form the backbone of the program can be used in parent training workshops to increase home literacy experiences or implemented by preschool teachers to enhance children's early reading skills. Alternatively, *Read with Me!* strategies can be taught directly to students in school settings or incorporated into intervention to help children with communication disorders increase their proficiency in both language and literacy skills.

GOALS

The *Read with Me!* program works to build language and literacy skills in a stress-free and fun manner. The primary goals include:

- Increasing awareness of the relationship between language and literacy
- Building the language and literacy skills of children with and without communication disorders
- Facilitating increases in literacy by making reading an enjoyable experience for all readers

In addition, each variation of the *Read with Me!* program targets specific goals. These goals are specified in the discussion of each variation (see Sections I–IV).

PROGRAM VARIATIONS

Although the *Read with Me!* program was originally created to increase the quality of home literacy experiences for preschool and young school-age children through direct parent training, the wide applicability of the *Read with Me!* strategies and philosophies quickly became apparent. This resource provides specific information regarding the organization and delivery of four variations of the *Read with Me!* program: (1) Home, (2) Older Children, (3) School, and (4) Speech-Language Intervention.

All the variations are based on the fundamental *Read with Me!* philosophy that stresses the importance of engaging children in the reading experience and keeping the interaction highly rewarding to the participants. However, each variation is unique in that it targets a specific age group or delivery system. Note that the variations are not mutually exclusive. That is, parents could be attending Home workshops while their children are participating in School tutoring sessions. However, you do not have to implement all the variations of the programs described in this manual. You may choose to start with a Home program and explore the other components at a later time. Alternatively, you could choose to use the strategies with individual children within the context of speech-language intervention only. It all depends on your setting and the needs of your students. This flexibility makes *Read with Me!* a powerful tool for building language and literacy skills for all children

Read with Me! at Home

The Home variation teaches parents and educators of preschool children with and without identified disabilities how to improve early reading experiences in the home environment. (These strategies are also very appropriate for implementation in preschool settings.) The six basic *Read with Me!* strategies (see *"Read with Me!* Strategies," page 10) are taught through a series of highly interactive workshops that provide participants with hands-on experiences regarding these four topics:

1. Helping young children become more actively involved in reading
2. Selecting appropriate books
3. Modeling good reading behaviors
4. Making reading a fun and stress-free experience for all participants

Section I: Home provides organization and management information, lesson plans, facilitator notes, and handouts that make it easy to implement a Home program in any setting.

Read with Me! for Older Children

This application of the *Read with Me!* program grew out of parents' and educators' requests for an extension of the use of the six *Read with Me!* strategies to older children (i.e., children who are beyond second grade). It was also developed in response to queries about how to encourage children who had become "reluctant readers" to become more engaged in reading activities. Section II: Older Children provides a lesson plan and handouts that address reading with older children.

Although useful for all older readers, this variation is especially valuable for those children whom, whatever the reason, might not have learned to love literature during their early reading experiences. This material can be used as stand-alone information or as an optional additional session for participants in a Home program.

Read with Me! in School

This variation provides preschool and kindergarten children with daily one-to-one tutoring in their school setting using the *Read with Me!* strategies discussed under *"Read with Me!* Strategies" (see page 10), plus instruction involving poetry and chapter books. Because many children who have language and communication delays experience related delays in reading, a School program can be especially beneficial in helping build skills in both domains.

To accomplish this, facilitators (who may be either professional educators or trained volunteers) conduct one-to-one, 15-minute sessions each day for qualified students. In addition, carryover to the home environment is provided through demonstration videotapes. Periodically, each child takes home a book and a videotape of themselves reading that book with a facilitator using one of the *Read with Me!* strategies. Section III: School provides organization and management information, facilitator notes, handouts, videotape scripts, and record-keeping forms for School programs.

Read with Me! in Speech-Language Intervention

The basic strategies and highly engaging books used in the *Read with Me!* program are extremely appropriate and adaptable for use in clinical applications for children with a variety of communication disorders. Since *Read with Me!* is founded on the premise of a strong relationship between language and literacy, the infinite possibilities for application to therapeutic goals becomes quickly apparent.

Section IV: Speech-Language Intervention provides examples of how the *Read with Me!* strategies and recommended books can be used to meet a variety of goals and objectives related to communication disorders. Use these examples as a springboard for generating intervention goals.

BACKGROUND
General

Researchers and educators agree that children who are competent in oral and written language are at a distinct advantage, both in school and in community activities, over children who have not developed these critical skills (U.S Department of Education, 2000). Children who do not develop proficiency in talking, reading, and writing often experience related problems in daily communication, social skills, and academic content areas such as math, social studies, and science (Fey, Catts, and Larrivee, 1995).

Most people believe that children go to school to learn to read. However, a recent report by the Institute of Child Health and Human Development (2002) indicated that in order to become good readers, children must develop certain foundational skills related to literacy before formal reading instruction begins in school. Many skills have been identified as key components to becoming a good reader, such as understanding sound-symbol relationships, sound segmentation, and sound blending (Adams, 1990; Blachman, 1994). While these abilities are certainly important, the strategies and techniques associated with the *Read with Me!* program are designed to target skills that are even more crucial to the development of literacy.

Steven Bialostok, in his book *Raising Readers* (1992), listed nine stages through which a child must progress to become an independent reader. These stages are:

1. Learning to love books
2. Enjoying the meaning of books
3. Learning how books work
4. Discovering that print has meaning
5. Memorizing books
6. Rehearsing books
7. Recognizing the words
8. Developing fluency
9. Reading independently

Note that the primary focus of formal reading instruction is on the last three stages. Clearly, children who come to school with a solid understanding of the fundamental skills associated with the first six stages have a substantial head start on the reading game.

Jim Trelease, in *The New Read-Aloud Handbook* (1989), stressed that the most important thing parents can do to help their children develop literacy skills is to help them develop a desire to read. Too often, children develop a "reading is work" (p. 24) mentality because adults attempt to teach them to read before they teach them to know the joy of reading. Trelease argued that the all-important desire to read is not born in the child. Rather, "it is planted there by parents and teachers who work at it" (p. 24).

Parents, as children's first and most influential teachers, are in a position to provide the fundamental literacy experiences that can open the doors for their children to become lifelong readers. The good news is that teaching parents to use certain techniques during storybook reading supports the development of their children's expressive language skills as well as advances literacy skills (Snow, Burns, and Griffin, 1998). In fact, parent-child storybook reading has been described by many researchers as an ideal, natural context for facilitating these important skills (Crowe, Norris, and Hoffman, 2000).

The bad news is that merely directing parents to "read to your child" is not enough. Parents need to understand why reading with their child is important, how to read effectively, and what kinds of children's literature support the development of language and early reading skills. If we wish to maximize the benefits of a child's reading experiences, parents must be provided with strategies that support the development of specific skills. In addition, parents need to experience how a reading interaction can be an exciting and rewarding adventure for both participants, rather than a chore to be checked off a parent's already exhaustive "to-do" list.

Applications to Specific Populations

One of the most exciting aspects of this program is that it can be easily adapted for use across a wide variety of applications. The strategies, books, and philosophies described in this resource have been shared with families and teachers of children who are developing typically, children who are late talkers, children with language delays, children with autism, children with hearing loss, children with cognitive delays, children from low socioeconomic status (SES) homes, and children from English as a second language (ESL) families. In addition, the strategies included in this program are appropriate for children as young as 12 months until well into the elementary school years. Families and educators of children who are developing typically and families of children with various developmental delays can participate in the same workshops and learn the same techniques, side by side, and adapt them to meet the needs of their children.

Children Who Are Developing Typically

Research by Robertson, Smith, and Sollenberger (2001) suggested that typically developing children whose parents participated in *Read with Me!* training attended to the reading interaction longer, used more verbal interaction, and demonstrated more complex language during the reading interaction compared to children whose parents did not receive the training. In addition, parents of the children in the experimental group demonstrated a statistically significant increase in the percentage of open-ended questions they used during story interactions as well as a decrease in the amount of time they talked in proportion to the amount of time children talked.

In addition, the parents studied reported that their children's attitudes toward book reading were positively affected as demonstrated by variables such as an increased eagerness to read, an increase in the number of minutes read per session, and an increase in children's willingness to talk about books. See Appendix A, *Parent Literacy Training Study*, for a synopsis of this data.

The U.S. Department of Education (2000) in collaboration with the Institute of Child Health and Human Development identified a number of core skills that children need to develop in order to be effective readers. Included in this list are phonemic awareness, vocabulary development, fluency, and text comprehension. Development of these critical skills is facilitated through consistent use of the strategies that make up the *Read with Me!* program. In addition, by keeping reading interactions fun and stress-free, everyone involved in the reading interaction can relax and enjoy the experience. In this way, *Read with Me!* helps children learn to read and learn to love to read!

Children with Communication Disorders

The language and literacy development of children with communication disorders—such as late talkers, children with language delays, children with autism, children with hearing loss, or children with cognitive delays—can be positively affected by the implementation of *Read with Me!* strategies and the use of the recommended books. In fact, given the close relationship between language and literacy, early exposure to appropriate reading experiences is especially essential to children with delays in the linguistic domain (Kahmi and Catts, 1986).

Longitudinal follow-up studies, in which children with language delays were followed from early preschool through the primary grades, have consistently found that children with a history of language impairments are at substantial risk for reading disabilities (Bishop and Adams, 1990; Catts, 1993; Magnusson and Naucler, 1990; Silva, Williams, and McGee, 1985; Stark et al., 1984). Although not all children with histories of early language delay eventually demonstrate delays in written language, the results of these studies indicated that between 40–85% of these youngsters will experience problems related to reading and writing.

There are a number of theories that have attempted to explain the relationship between language impairment and constrained or delayed reading achievement. Some researchers have speculated that children with language disorders may have a fundamental problem processing incoming information (Ellis Weismer, 1996). If this is the case, providing parents with strategies and techniques that make the reading interaction more salient to children is crucial to children's eventual successes in both the linguistic and literacy domains.

Alternatively, the transactional model of language development (Yoder and Warren, 1993) suggests that the learning process involves ongoing reciprocal interactions between child behaviors and parent behaviors. Early disruption in the development of children's language systems can have a negative effect on the dynamics of this interaction, reducing the potential for learning to occur in a natural social context. Preschoolers with language impairments may not respond to parent-child reading experiences in the same way as children who are developing typically. This may, in turn, make the reading interactions between parent and child less enjoyable to the parent, who may respond by reducing the time and frequency of reading with the child. This results in fewer opportunities for children to engage in the very experiences that build language and literacy skills.

Similarly, school-aged children who have the most difficulty reading are given the least opportunity to actually engage in reading experiences. Rather, a preponderance of their reading time is spent on reading skills instruction (Trelease, 1989). While this is not inherently bad, it does not provide children with opportunities to learn to enjoy reading (i.e., to develop a desire to read for the sake of reading). This can lead to a negative spiral in which children with language-learning difficulties fall further and further behind as they become less and less involved in the reading experience.

From either perspective, children with language-based learning difficulties are especially in need of enhanced literacy-building experiences. Providing parents and teachers of children who have communication difficulties with clear directives on how to read to children can result in a more effective, and a more enjoyable, experience for all participants. Children who have been encouraged to become active participants in reading experiences are likely to demonstrate an increase in their oral vocabulary and language skills as well as behaviors related to literacy. *(Read with Me!* facilitators might also want to consider a complementary resource called *Talk! Talk! Talk!* [Muir et al., 2000], which provides strategies for developing children's speaking and listening skills.)

READ WITH ME! STRATEGIES

When young children are actively involved in the reading process, they take ownership of the literature and soon consider themselves to be "readers." All variations of the *Read with Me!* program target six specific strategies and incorporate literature genres that encourage young readers to become more fully engaged in the reading interaction. These strategies are taught separately to the program participants, but in face-to-face interactions with children, they may be combined.

Echo Reading

This very simple strategy encourages children to begin to understand that what is written on the page matches the words that are produced orally. Although it is not a natural strategy, it is an easily taught and highly effective method of actively including even very young children in the reading interaction—so that adults are reading *with* children, not just *to* them.

Using this strategy, the adult reads a short phrase and then asks the child to repeat what was read by using prompts, such as "Copy me" or "Say what I say." Books that are most appropriate for echo reading have short, simple phrases (generally one per page) complemented by highly engaging and child-friendly illustrations and story lines. This strategy can also be used with children who have begun to develop literacy skills. Echo reading with an adult helps these emerging readers learn a book quickly and gain confidence in their ability to eventually read the story independently.

Paired Reading

Paired reading (sometimes referred to as *shared reading*) is a very natural strategy. The adult reads part of a phrase (or book or story) and the child then takes a turn and "reads" another part. Through the effective use of pausing, intonation, and stress, adults signal to the child that it is his or her turn to "read." Books with repetitive, predictable, and/or rhyming phrases allow pre-readers to anticipate what is coming next and chime in with confidence.

Invite children to participate by selecting books that are appropriate for each child's age and interests as well as books that support the use of a paired reading strategy. However, once children are "hooked" on a book, it is almost impossible to stop them from taking their turns! This is an effective and fun technique for helping children become happy and confident readers.

Questioning

It is best if parents and educators use an open-ended (i.e., "friendly") question style that encourages children to think critically about the story, to use more complex language, and to reduce the pressure that often results when there is just one "right" answer. While there is a time and place to use fact-based (i.e., "scary") questions to monitor comprehension, very young children should not be "drilled" about the story, even when adults mean well.

Parents and educators know that they should ask questions during reading interactions, but they do not always consider the type of questions they are asking. Most are astonished, and often somewhat chagrined, when they realize how many fact-based questions they are asking children. In fact, when investigating the effectiveness of this program, prior to training, every parent asked more fact-based than open-ended questions during reading interactions with their children—with the majority of parents using fact-based questions exclusively (100% of the time)!

Time and time again, participants in *Read with Me!* workshops say that it was this strategy that really changed their thinking about reading with children. For some adults, learning about this strategy is something of an epiphany as they realize that perhaps this was why they did not enjoy reading as a child—because they often felt stressed and unhappy when they could not answer the questions correctly. We can all relate to the feeling of sitting in class and not knowing the answer and hoping that the teacher did not call on us. However, if you are the only child in the interaction, you know you are going to be called on. By accepting all answers, adults encourage children to verbally participate in the interaction without fear that they might say the "wrong" thing. One of the authors always lets parents know that this is the strategy that had the greatest influence on her interactions with young children—in both reading interactions and in conversation.

In addition to reducing stress, open-ended questions encourage children to produce longer verbalizations and use more complex language than merely answering with a rote response (which tends to be one or two words in length). Compare the answer a child might give to the following questions:

- **Q:** What color is Mary's dress? (fact-based, "scary" question)
  A: Red.
- **Q:** Why do you think Mary is wearing a red dress? (open-ended, "friendly" question)
  A: It's her favorite color.

Another reason to encourage the use of open-ended questions is to help children use their critical thinking skills. The development of good thinking skills is extremely important to the academic and, eventually, the vocational success of children. Unfortunately, many teachers express their concern about the inability of children in their classrooms to solve problems by using their thinking skills. Adults can help children develop these skills by using strategies, such as open-ended questions, that facilitate these important competencies. For instance, the adult can ask different questions each time a book is read to encourage children to think differently about the characters, the action, and the consequences of the story.

Although all children can benefit when adults employ more "friendly" questions in their reading interactions, it is especially important to encourage parents and educators of children with language delays or disorders to use these questioning strategies. Because these children are at risk for developing effective literacy skills, they are in particular need of opportunities to help them discover the joy of reading. In addition, friendly questions encourage children to build language skills by facilitating longer and more complex verbalizations.

Predicting

This strategy is presented as a complement to the questioning strategy. Both strategies target increasing language and critical thinking skills, as well as encouraging children to actively participate in the reading interaction.

Since predicting in its purest form is available only the first time a book is read, adults must read a new book through in its entirety before they read it with a child to determine if it has good potential as a prediction story. Some books provide visual prediction cues about what might happen next in the story (e.g., *The Mitten*). For others, children must rely on the words of the story only (e.g., *If You Give a Mouse a Cookie*) and their own imagination to help them predict the next event. Both types of books are excellent resources for building language and thinking skills.

Wordless Books

Wordless books help children discover that what they say can be written and what is written can be read. The use of wordless books as vehicles for adult-child interaction related to literacy is especially appropriate for parents who are not proficient in English as well as those who are not literate.

With wordless books, children (and adults) are not hampered by a set story line, so they are able to become the "author" of the story and tell it any way they wish. Children also gain experience in sequencing, thinking skills, predicting, and editing. Wordless books help children learn to read without words!

Reader's Theatre

This strategy capitalizes on a child's natural interest in dramatic play by encouraging children to engage their whole bodies and minds in a story. Reader's theatre can be as simple as a fingerplay, such as *Five Little Monkeys*, or as complicated as creating a dramatic representation of the story using puppets or even commercial props.

Children who are at risk for an impoverished or delayed development of dramatic play skills, such as children with autism and children with language disorders, can particularly benefit from practicing play in the familiar and safe environment of adult-child reading interactions.

HOW TO USE THE PROGRAM

Not all the strategies and books recommended in *Read with Me!* are equally effective or appropriate for all adult-child reading pairs. It is always fun to hear parents and teachers talk about which books their children loved, but sometimes they also talk about books they did not enjoy! Encourage participants to use a combination of strategies and literature that works for their child/students and for their family/classroom. Remind participants that they should never force a child to read a book or use a strategy that the child does not like. Although information for a number of books is provided for use with *Read with Me!* strategies and genres, the list of all possible choices is much larger. (See Appendix B, *Expanded Book Lists.*) Regardless of the setting or age level, the primary directive is to always keep the reading interaction fun and stress free.

No specialized training is required to implement the *Read with Me!* program. In fact, everything you need to know is provided for you in this resource. It is best, however, that the program coordinator be a certified educator with expertise in the areas of language and literacy. Generally, this would be a speech-language pathologist, reading specialist, or early childhood educator. However, a facilitator can be anyone who has a strong interest in working with young children and has a good working knowledge of, or experience with, the *Read with Me!* strategies. You may adapt the programs however you wish to fit the needs of your setting and the children with whom you work.

The accompanying CD-ROM provides a PowerPoint presentation (as well as reproducible individual slides) that is very effective to use during parent or facilitator training sessions. The slide program clearly illustrates the focus of *Read with Me!* and the importance of early literacy skills. In addition, the CD-ROM provides all the reproducible materials in the book so that readers can conveniently print out pages.

MEASURING PROGRESS

The *Read with Me!* Home and School sections provide specific pre/post evaluation forms for documenting changes that occur as a result of engaging children in the reading strategies. These two sections contain reproducible forms plus guidelines for when to use which form. The results should be shared with any individuals or agencies who are "stockholders" in the successful implementation of *Read with Me!*

Section I

Home

Read with Me!

CONTENTS

Overview 17
Goals 18
Organization 18
Staff Training 18
Funding 18
Recruitment 20
Program Delivery 20
Lesson Plans and Books 20
Data Collection 21
Session 1: Echo Reading and Paired Reading 22
Session 2: Questioning and Predicting 29
Session 3: Wordless Books and Reader's Theatre 37
Pre/Post Survey 45
Effective Reading Techniques for Young Readers 47
How to Include Children in Echo Reading and Paired Reading .. 48
Reading Log 49
"Alexander" Quiz 50
Fun and Stress-Free Cue Card 51
Building Thinking Skills 52
The Kiss 53
Using Wordless Books to Increase Thinking Skills 54
Building Language and Literacy Skills with Reader's Theatre . 55
Joining the Literacy Club 56
If You Give a Child a Book 58
Final Project Evaluation 59

Section I

OVERVIEW

The *Read with Me!* Home program trains parents and educators how to use the six *Read with Me!* strategies to help young children become more fully engaged in the reading experience. Although initially designed as a program for parents of preschoolers, the strategies are actually appropriate for youngsters to the age of 8 and beyond. The program is not intended to be a type of, or alternate to, formal reading instruction, but rather a vehicle for building the foundational skills and experiences that are critical to a child's development as a literate individual. Building on the premise that reading with preschoolers should be fun and stress free, the strategies are shared through a series of workshops that can be tailored to the needs of the group that is participating. This training has been provided for parents of children with and without special needs, for general-education classroom teachers, for Head Start teachers, for preschool teachers, for graduate students in speech-language pathology, and at "trainer of trainers" (i.e., a facilitator can train others to be facilitators) workshops.

Examples of children's literature that facilitate the use of each of the six strategies are shared with participants. Even preschoolers, who are not yet developmentally ready to read, can become actively involved in reading when adults know how to use these strategies and how to choose literature that facilitates their use. Participants learn that children learn to read by being read to, but they keep reading because they learn to love to read.

Results of a study undertaken to test the efficacy of the *Read with Me!* Home program demonstrated robust positive changes in both child and adult behaviors during reading interactions (Robertson et al., 2001). Children whose parents participated in *Read with Me!* training attended to the reading interaction longer, used more verbal interaction, and demonstrated more complex language during the reading interaction compared to children whose parents did not receive the training. In addition, parents of the children in the experimental group demonstrated a statistically significant increase in the percentage of open-ended questions they used during story interactions as well as a decrease in the amount of time the adult talked in proportion to the amount of time the child talked. See Appendix A for a synopsis of the data.

In addition, of more than 150 families who have participated in various *Read with Me!* workshops, 100% reported positive changes in their children's attitudes toward book reading as measured by the pre/post instrument found on page 45. Parents reported that their children demonstrated an increased eagerness to read, an increase in the number of minutes read per session, and an increase in their willingness to talk about books. Many parents self-reported a positive increase in their own confidence and pleasure in reading with their children.

Read with Me!

GOALS

- Facilitate participant's understanding of the importance of reading together to the language and literacy development of children ages 1–8.
- Provide participants with methods to promote active child participation during reading interactions in the home environment.
- Introduce participants to a wide variety of children's literature that supports the development of critical language and literacy skills.

ORGANIZATION

The first rule in organizing a Home program is to realize that you probably cannot do it alone. You will want to solicit the support of your administration, teachers, colleagues, parent groups, and so on in order to provide a program that is most effective (and to preserve your sanity). However, the organization and implementation of the program is not difficult. Everything you need to implement a Home program is provided, including detailed lesson plans and handouts.

STAFF TRAINING

One of the first things you may want to do is introduce fellow educators and staff to the program. This serves two purposes. In the best case scenario (and this actually happens a lot), you will very likely find that staff members become so excited about the program that they will actually volunteer to help you implement it. Alternatively, they will at least know what you are doing so that when parents talk to them, they will understand the program and its philosophy.

Consider training staff in one session, using a compressed version of the lesson plans presented later in this section. Tailor the session to meet particular needs, but go over each of the strategies and demonstrate them with a few books. This session usually takes about one to two hours. Giving the *"Alexander" Quiz* (see page 50) is always beneficial because it teaches participants how to ask questions that foster language and literacy.

FUNDING

This program can be implemented with a relatively small budget. You will need to purchase books to use as instructional materials (it is recommended that you purchase Big Books whenever possible) as well as a few other small items. Purchasing information for the books

Section I

recommended in this resource can be found in Appendix C. Generally, these start-up costs run approximately $500 for 20 participants. In addition, try to provide participants with a few free books. Light refreshments and childcare are recommended to encourage participation. A sample start-up budget, including instructor materials and optional participant materials for 20 participants, is outlined in Figure 1.1.

Figure 1.1   **Sample Start-Up Budget**

Instructor Materials

2 Big Books @ $10 each × 20 participants $400

20 additional books for demonstration @ $4 each $80

Materials for *Fun and Stress-Free Cue Card* $5

Big Book Stand $20

Post-it Notes $5

Name Tags $5

Copies (7 pages × 20 participants × $.05 per page) $7

TOTAL $522

Optional Participant Materials

2 books per session (total of 6) @ $4 each × 20 participants $480

Funding can come from a variety of sources; start with your administration. Literacy, especially family literacy, is gathering a great deal of support at the state and federal levels. Consequently, there may be funds available at the district level or even from your parent-teacher support group. Consider soliciting local businesses to help support the purchase of books. Other sources include local Rotary Clubs (whose national focus is now on building literacy), Title 1 funds designated for parent involvement, Even Start Grant Funds (*www.evenstart.org*), the Barbara Bush Family Literacy Foundation Grant (*www.barbarabushfoundation.com*), or the Coca-Cola Literacy Grant (404-676-2568). Keep your eyes open for potential sources and do not be afraid to ask.

RECRUITMENT

Your efforts to recruit parents from the local community will probably be most fruitful if you are able to contact parents directly to explain the program and its objectives. This can be undertaken at parent-teacher conferences, kindergarten and preschool orientation meetings, early childhood screenings, PTA meetings, open-house nights, and library story times. Sending flyers home with children can also be useful (but not as useful as direct contact). Try forming partnerships with your local preschools, Head Starts, or other regional agencies. Of course, many of you will have an active caseload and parents with whom you have already established a working relationship. This is an excellent population to target (you can always expand into the community once you have trained your own parents).

PROGRAM DELIVERY

Training parents and educators in the use of the *Read with Me!* strategies and philosophies is very flexible. It is presented here as a series of three sessions, one per week, of approximately 60–90 minutes each. However, you may wish to break the sessions down so that only one strategy is presented each week. Or you may need to compress the training, depending on your time and resources.

It is extremely important that you establish an informal, non-threatening environment whether you are presenting this information to parents or to your fellow educators. No one wants to be made to feel like he or she does not know how to parent or how to teach. Consequently, it is very important not to come across as the "expert." Rather, you want to help participants in the workshop feel like they are doing lots of things right already, but now they are learning how to do those things more deliberately, more effectively, and with more confidence.

It is best to have at least two people facilitate the sessions. With two presenters, the workshops can be facilitated in a more casual manner. One "teacher" alone tends to lecture, where two can enter into a conversation that communicates the information in a less threatening manner.

LESSON PLANS AND BOOKS

Three detailed lesson plans for the Home sessions are provided beginning on page 22. Each of the three lesson plans provides a suggested materials list, step-by-step directions for sharing the strategies and books, facilitator notes, and handouts. You may reproduce the handouts (from the book or the accompanying CD-ROM) for use in presenting the sessions to parents and educators. The most important aspect of the program is a spirit of collaboration and adventure, so do not be afraid to add your own touches or favorite books. You will note that the generic term *participants* is used in place of *parents* or *teachers* because the sessions are equally valuable to both groups.

Detailed references and purchasing information for all the books listed in the lesson plans can be found in Appendix B and Appendix C, respectively. These lists are not all-inclusive. However, a cross-section of the types of books that support the targeted strategies most effectively is provided. You will find your own favorites.

DATA COLLECTION

We suggest that you make an attempt to gather data to support your efforts. At a minimum, have participants keep a *Reading Log* (see page 49) and complete either a *Pre/Post Training Survey* (see page 45) or a *Final Project Evaluation* (see page 59). Consider using incentives (e.g., bonus books) as a means of encouraging participants to return these documents. Use the information obtained from surveys and evaluations to plan future sessions with participants.

Read with Me!

Session 1
Echo Reading and Paired Reading

MATERIALS

- Participant packet (a pocket folder works well to organize information) containing:
  Name tag
  Pre/Post Survey (see page 45)
  Effective Reading Techniques for Young Readers (see page 47)
  How to Include Children in Echo Reading and Paired Reading (see page 48)
  Reading Log (see page 49)

- Big Book stand

- Recommended books for demonstration (use Big Books if possible; see Appendix B for a complete reference for each book listed):
  I Went Walking
  Dinosaur Roar!
  Bears in Pairs
  In the Small, Small Pond
  Time for Bed
  Silly Sally
  Dinosaur Stomp
  The Very Busy Spider/The Very Quiet Cricket/The Very Lonely Firefly
  One Duck Stuck

- Other echo reading and paired reading books to display (see Appendix B)

- Optional (but recommended) items:
  Overhead Presentation (see Appendix D)
  Copies of books for participants
  Refreshments

Section I

LESSON PLAN
Opening

1. See "Facilitator's Notes" (page 27) for preparation.
2. Hand out the participant packets.
3. Have participants complete the *Pre/Post Survey* (see page 45).
4. Have participants share a reading memory (good or bad). Be prepared to share one of your own. State that the goal is for the children that participants read with to be able to recall many happy memories related to reading.
5. Discuss the importance and purposes of reading with children. (The *Overhead Presentation* provided in Appendix D and on the accompanying CD-ROM provides an overview of the relationship between language and literacy and the importance of early reading experiences.) Cover the following points:
    - Reading with children builds language skills that are essential to learning to read and write.
    - Reading with children helps prepare them for formal reading instruction.
    - Reading with children encourages them to become readers by learning to love to read.
6. Explain that two specific strategies (how to read) and books that work well with the targeted strategies (what to read) will be shared at each workshop. Encourage participants to be active members of the session—stress the idea of a collaborative workshop rather than a "sit and get" format.
7. Discuss the idea that how participants read with children is as important as how much they read. Go over the suggestions on *Effective Reading Techniques for Young Readers* (see page 47). You may just want to give an overview instead of having participants read along with you point by point. When you feel that participants are ready to move on, say:

    Now, that we are all on the same page regarding reading together with children, it's time to learn about the first Read with Me! *strategy!*

8. Have the Big Book stand ready to display books as you talk about them.

Echo Reading
Introduce the Strategy

Explain that when echo reading, the adult reads a short phrase and then asks the child to repeat what was read by using prompts such as "Copy me" or "Say what I say." While using echo reading, tell participants they should point to each word as it is read (by either the adult or child).

Read with Me!

Point out that this is one of the easiest and most effective strategies to teach children. However, it does not come naturally to many children—or to adults! This strategy often must be taught directly to children.

Tell participants that echo reading helps a child begin to understand that the words in the book match the words that come out of our mouths. It can be used with very young children (18 months) as well as with older children (at least until age 7). The amount of echoing may vary, but the purpose is the same—to get the child actively engaged in the reading experience.

Demonstrate the Strategy with a Specific Book

Use the story *I Went Walking* (or one of the books listed under "Share Additional Books That Support the Strategy," page 25) and:

1. State that the best way to explain the strategy is just to demonstrate it.
2. Tell participants that they will be the children ("echoers"). Then say "Copy me!"
3. Point to the words on the first page as you read them and say "I went walking." If you have more than one facilitator, have one facilitator read and another echo back the words to encourage participants to join in.
4. Look at participants expectantly until they echo "I went walking."
5. Continue this procedure for a few pages.
6. Leaf through the rest of the story, and talk about how the child "loses" clothing as he proceeds through the book. He actually ends up with it all again at the end—which is, of course, nothing like a normal child!

Clarify Proper Use of the Strategy

Explain that with younger children, or children who have difficulty attending, it is best to have them echo smaller chunks of text. Some children may do this naturally. Give an example such as the following:

ADULT: I went walking.
CHILD: Walking

Older children can generally handle larger chunks of text (but not always).

Tell participants to accept whatever response a child gives. Emphasize that they should not correct the child. If a child is consistently repeating a phrase incorrectly (e.g., "What you did see?" rather than "What did you see?"), the best strategy is for the adult to emphasize the correct word order when reading (e.g., What *did you* see?).

Section I

Share Additional Books That Support the Strategy

Share at least two to three additional books to ensure that participants understand the strategy and the kinds of books that support its use. Echo read, having participants repeat what you read for the first few pages of each book. Then leaf through the rest of the book, pointing out salient details. The following books are recommended for practice:

Dinosaur Roar!

1. Talk about the rich vocabulary.
2. Note the use of unusual opposites (such as *clean* and *slimy* versus *clean* and *dirty*).
3. Point out the wonderful, eye-catching pictures and the natural appeal of dinosaurs.
4. Share that this is one of the most naturally appealing books to use. Many children inherently respond to the friendly dinosaurs and catchy text.

Bears in Pairs

1. Point out the great descriptive vocabulary.
2. Note the opposites—some unexpected and unusual.
3. Notice that all the bear "pairs" can be found at the tea party at the end of the book.

In the Small, Small Pond

1. Note that this book is also rich in vocabulary, even though there are only a few words on each page.
2. Talk about the rhyme and alliteration (i.e., words that start with the same sounds).
3. Point out the outstanding illustrations.

Paired Reading

Introduce the Strategy

Explain that when pair reading, the adult reads part of a phrase (or book or story) and the child then takes a turn and "reads" another part. Through the effective use of pausing, intonation, and stress, adults signal to the child that it is his or her turn to "read." Tell participants that paired reading is a more natural strategy than echo reading for both adults and children.

Demonstrate the Strategy with a Specific Book

Use the story *Time for Bed* (or one of the books listed under "Share Additional Books That Support the Strategy," page 26) and:

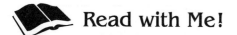 **Read with Me!**

1. State that the best way to explain the strategy is to demonstrate it.
2. Tell participants that they will be the children.
3. Talk about and demonstrate how to use pausing and intonation to indicate that it is the child's turn to "read."
4. Point out that this book provides great vocabulary input. It covers the names of many baby animals (e.g., a baby horse is a *foal*, not a *pony*) and the sounds they make. Also, the strong rhyming component makes this book especially good for paired reading.

Clarify Proper Use of the Strategy

Say something like:

> *You should read the book with the child at least five times before expecting him or her to begin to chime in. Just like with echo reading, don't force the child to talk. If you pause and the child doesn't chime in the expected words, say them yourself and move on.*

Share Additional Books That Support the Strategy

Share at least two to three additional books to ensure that participants understand the strategy and the kinds of books that support its use. Have participants chime in on the repetitive phrases or rhyming sections for at least the first few pages of the additional books that you demonstrate. Then leaf through the rest of the book, pointing out salient details. The following books are recommended for practice:

Silly Sally

1. Point out how the repetitive phrase "…backwards upside down" is ideal for pairing and it is silly and fun! (This keeps children's interest levels high.)
2. Share that many participants have indicated that this book is one that children respond to very quickly.

Dinosaur Stomp

Consider reading the entire book aloud with participants using the paired reading technique.

The Very Busy Spider, The Very Quiet Cricket, or *The Very Lonely Firefly*

Consider sharing at least one of these books by Eric Carle. Each has a repetitive phrase that is great for paired reading, rich vocabulary, and a fun gimmick.

One Duck Stuck

1. Point out the repetitive phrases "Help, help. Who can help?" and "No luck. Still stuck!"
2. Note that the counting is just a bonus and should not be the focus of the reading interaction.

Closing

1. Go over *How to Include Children in Echo Reading and Paired Reading* (see page 48).
2. Direct participants' attention to *Expanded Book Lists* (Appendix B) for additional books that support echo reading and paired reading. Make copies of the appropriate sections of Appendix B for participants.
3. Tell participants to examine the *Reading Log* (see page 49), and encourage them to record books they read with children for all sessions.
4. Invite questions (See Appendix E, *Frequently Asked Questions*).
5. Solicit participant suggestions for other books that could support the echo reading or paired reading strategies.
6. Thank participants for coming and emphasize that you hope to see them back next week for two new strategies.
7. Optional: Invite participants to have some refreshments and look over the books you have on display.

FACILITATOR'S NOTES
General Considerations

The way the first session is presented sets the tone for the remaining sessions. The sessions were designed to be collaborative in nature. You need to guard against coming across as the "expert." Rather, you want participants to feel like their input is valuable and that they are to be commended for participating.

Tell parents and educators that they are probably already using many of the strategies you will discuss. This helps participants feel less defensive about learning new things. This is especially important when you are working with educators. Stress that the point of the session is to help parents and educators become more aware of why these strategies work and how to purposely use them to increase language and literacy skills.

Make the point that you are very interested in hearing about how the strategies work for participants' children/students. Ask for feedback at the beginning and end of each of the sessions. Use this feedback along with information obtained from the *Pre/Post Surveys* to plan future sessions with participants.

In addition, stress that you not only want to share the strategies, you want to share the books that are especially good for each strategy. Point out that part of the fun is learning what to read as well as how to read more effectively with children.

Special Considerations for Working with Educators

Due to time constraints, you may consider compressing the three sessions into one session when working with educators. However, many educators may wish to attend multiple sessions as parents.

You may also need to address why a speech-language pathologist (if that is who happens to be facilitating the session) is training educators about reading. Generally, once you describe the relationship between language and learning (consider using the *Overhead Presentation* found in Appendix D), this question answers itself. Sometimes, however, it is not a bad idea for the facilitator to ask and answer the question (e.g., "You may be wondering why a speech-language pathologist is talking about reading. The best way to answer that question is to demonstrate the strong link that exists between language and literacy." Then proceed with the overhead presentation).

Finally, it is a good idea to add information about how the reading experiences associated with rhythm and rhyme, as found in most echo reading and paired reading interactions, help build skills in the area of phonemic awareness. (Do not overemphasize this with parents; you do not want them to be tempted to become reading teachers instead of reading facilitators.)

Session 2
Questioning and Predicting

MATERIALS

- *Alexander and the Terrible, Horrible, No Good, Very Bad Day*

- *"Alexander" Quiz* (see page 50)

- *Fun and Stress-Free Cue Card* (see page 51)

- Big Book stand

- Recommended minimum books for demonstration (use Big Books if possible, except for *Alexander and the Terrible, Horrible, No Good, Very Bad Day*; see Appendix B for a complete reference for each book listed):
  Mary Wore Her Red Dress
  The Little Mouse, the Red Ripe Strawberry, and the Big Hungry Bear
  Today I Feel Silly and Other Moods That Make My Day
  I Went Walking
  Is Your Mama a Llama?
  Look! Look! Look!
  If You Give a Moose a Muffin/If You Give a Mouse a Cookie/If You Give a Pig a Pancake
  Rosie's Walk
  Bark, George!
  Dos and Don'ts
  The Mitten

- *Building Thinking Skills* (see page 52)

- Other questioning and predicting books to display (see Appendix B)

- Optional (but recommended) items:
  Copies of books for participants
  Refreshments

Read with Me!

LESSON PLAN

Opening

1. See "Facilitator's Notes" (see page 34) for preparation.
2. Encourage participants to share their experiences at home using last week's strategies. Did they work? Which books did children especially enjoy? Did they find other books that worked well using these strategies?
3. Explain to participants that this week two additional strategies will be demonstrated—asking good questions and making predictions. Tell participants that both of these strategies can be used with most of the books you have already talked about, but that you are going to share more books that are especially good for these new strategies.
4. Say to participants:

    Before we get started, I want to read you a story. Now, it is very important that you listen very carefully to the story. Even if you already know this story, you need to listen very carefully!

5. Read *Alexander and the Terrible, Horrible, No Good, Very Bad Day.* Make the point repeatedly that participants need to listen very carefully. Remind participants at intervals throughout the story that you want to make sure they understand that they are to listen.
6. Give the *"Alexander" Quiz* (see page 50). Ask questions quickly and forcefully. Ask specific people. Require specific answers. Be a bit nasty!
7. Have the Big Book stand ready to display books as you talk about them.

Questioning

Introduce Strategy

Use the last question of the *"Alexander" Quiz* to elicit participant responses regarding how they felt during this activity. (You are looking for words such as *pressured, stressed out, uncomfortable,* and *unhappy*). Emphasize that, without meaning to, adults often make reading a less than enjoyable experience because they ask only factual questions—questions that have only one right and very specific answer. This tends to make children less apt to want to read, resist answering questions, and less than efficient thinkers. Remind participants that reading should be fun and stress free (hold up the *Fun and Stress-Free Cue Card*).

Tell participants that they want to encourage children to think for themselves. Fact-based questions (consider calling these "scary" questions when speaking with parents) do not help children learn to use their critical thinking skills. These skills are vitally important for success in school and in life, but we do not always take the time to help children develop them properly.

Section I

Stress that instead of asking fact-based questions, participants want to ask questions that help children think and reduce the stress that questions having only one right answer can cause. Explain that these are called open-ended questions (consider calling these "friendly" questions when speaking with parents). For the story about Alexander, you might ask:

- *How might you feel if you got gum in your hair?*
- *How do you feel when your day is not going right?*
- *Why do you think Alex talks about Australia all the time?*

Tell participants that if they want to ask a more factual question, they can add *think* to the question. For example:

- *What color do you THINK it is?*
- *Who do you THINK got to sit next to the window?*

State that open-ended questions also encourage children to use longer verbalizations and more complex language when answering. This helps build the language and vocabulary skills that are so important to learning. Keep emphasizing that the most important thing to remember when asking questions is to keep reading fun and stress free (hold up the *Fun and Stress-Free Cue Card*).

Demonstrate the Strategy with a Specific Book

Use the story *Mary Wore Her Red Dress* (or one of the books listed under "Share Additional Books That Support the Strategy," page 32) and:

1. Talk about how the story is not really in the words, but in the pictures.
2. On the first page, model one or two open-ended questions.
3. Then, for each of the following pages, have one or two participants suggest a good question.
4. Point out the silly things and slightly naughty situations the characters get into during the party. These situations stimulate many opportunities for open-ended questions.
5. Tell participants that paired reading can also be used while reading this book with a child.

Clarify Proper Use of the Strategy

Tell participants that they should ask only one or two questions per page. Point out that they can ask different questions when they read the book another time. Explain that participants do not have to ask questions on every page or every time they read a book. It is acceptable to just read the words sometimes.

Share Additional Books That Support the Strategy

Share at least two to three additional books to ensure that participants understand the strategy and the kinds of books that support its use. Model open-ended questions while reading each book. The following are recommended for practice:

The Little Mouse, the Red Ripe Strawberry, and the Big Hungry Bear

1. Point out the wonderful facial expressions on the mouse.
2. Have participants offer some model questions as appropriate.
3. Talk about the narrator's motive for getting some of the red, ripe strawberry.

Today I Feel Silly and Other Moods That Make My Day

Model and solicit open-ended questions as appropriate.

Predicting

Introduce the Strategy

Explain that another good way to help children learn to think for themselves and to use their best language is by using predicting techniques. Tell participants that they should always read a book themselves before reading the book to a child. Explain that if they do not preview a book first, they may not be aware of the prediction opportunities in the book.

Demonstrate the Strategy with a Specific Book

Use the story *I Went Walking* (or one of the books listed under "Share Additional Books That Support the Strategy," page 33) and:

Point out the prediction clues on each page (e.g., the kitty's tail peeking out of a basket) and explain that they could have been easily missed if participants were not looking for them.

Clarify Proper Use of the Strategy

Explain that some books provide visual prediction clues, while others require a child to use his or her imagination to think about what might happen next. Point out that many books lend themselves to both questioning and predicting strategies.

Share Additional Books That Support the Strategy

Share at least two to three additional books to ensure that participants understand the strategy and the kinds of books that support its use. Provide participants with opportunities to make predictions about a given story as you leaf through the book. You will rarely have time to go through the entire book, but do share enough to help participants get a feel for the story and the use of the strategy. The following books are recommend for practice:

Is Your Mama a Llama?

1. Explain that this book uses auditory predicting cues.
2. Point out that in this book, the adult might not want to show the child the picture until after he or she has made a prediction.
3. Read the first few prediction episodes, and have participants guess the correct answer to the riddle.

Look! Look! Look!

1. Point out that this book employs visual predicting cues.
2. Have participants make their best guesses. Accept all answers (e.g., "It could be a cantaloupe. Oh, it's a sheep!").

If You Give a Moose a Muffin, If You Give a Mouse a Cookie, or *If You Give a Pig a Pancake*

Consider sharing at least one of these books by Laura Numeroff. This series of books has no visual clues, so children have to think for themselves.

Rosie's Walk

1. Tell participants that this book is a favorite of many children and adults.
2. Point out that there are lots of great predicting opportunities because the fox keeps trying to catch Rosie, but never quite accomplishes his goal.
3. Remind participants that the strategies can be overlapped or combined by pointing out that the text of this book can be read using echo reading or paired reading strategies at the same time as using questioning and predicting strategies.

Bark, George!

1. Notice especially the mother dog's expressions as she becomes more and more exasperated with George.
2. Take time to predict what sound George might make next or what the doctor might pull out of George.

Read with Me!

Dos and Don'ts

1. Read the first few pages together, taking time to stress *do* and *don't*.
2. Encourage participants to predict a silly "don't" rule to go along with a "do" rule.

The Mitten

1. Present this book as an example of higher level predicting for children who are over the age of 4 years or are very interested in visual detail.
2. Explain that there are actually three stories going on at once: Nikki's story on the right, the main story in the middle, and the prediction of what is coming next on the left.

Closing

1. Go over *Building Thinking Skills* (see page 52) with participants.
2. Ask "What do you think about these strategies?"
3. Ask "What do you think might happen next week?"
4. Remind participants to keep reading fun and stress free (hold up the *Fun and Stress-Free Cue Card*).
5. Invite questions (See Appendix E).
6. Solicit participant suggestions for other books that could support the questioning and predicting strategies.
7. Thank participants for coming and encourage them to come back next week for more fun and two more strategies.
8. Optional: Invite participants to have some refreshments and look over the books you have on display.

FACILITATOR'S NOTES
The "Alexander" Quiz

The way you present this activity is critical not only to the success of this session but to the training in general. Here is where you either win over your audience, or you lose them altogether. You are setting up the whole premise of the fun and stress-free philosophy. This is not the time to be shy! To be most effective, you need to be a bit obnoxious.

Reading the Book

You need to be very forceful about telling participants (whether you are working with parents or educators) to listen while you read *Alexander and the Terrible, Horrible, No Good, Very Bad Day*. If there is more than one facilitator, all should be emphasizing the point. Use phrases such as:

- *Are you listening?*
- *I don't think the man in the back with the green shirt is listening very well.*
- *You need to listen to this part. It is very important!*
- *Listen carefully!*
- *Don't forget to listen!*
- [To each other] *I am not sure they are listening. What do you think?*

You might consider pointing at specific participants and announcing that this is a very important part of the story, so they need to listen to it very carefully.

Giving the Quiz

At the end of the story, announce that there is now going to be a quiz to find out if the audience was really listening. (Do not tell participants that they will be quizzed ahead of time.) Give the quiz orally, not in written form. Point at specific people and demand an answer immediately. If a participant is incorrect, tell him or her the correct answer and say something like "I *told* you to listen! You should know this!"

On the first question ("What did Alexander find in his breakfast cereal?"), you will often get a correct answer. Respond with, "Good! You were listening!" On the second question ("What did Nick find in his cereal box?"), do not accept anything other than "Jr. Undercover Agent ring." If the response is "ring," it is wrong. Tell participants so! On the third question ("Who had a seat by the window in the car?"), require and demand three names—"I need three names! Weren't you listening?"

You may want to snap your fingers to indicate you want a response quickly. Make general disparaging comments, such as "You aren't very good listeners are you?" When someone gets an answer correct, say something like, "Well, at least someone was listening!"

Finishing the Quiz

The final question, "How did this quiz make you feel?" is designed to elicit responses that indicate that the participants felt uncomfortable and unhappy. You are looking for someone to say

Read with Me!

the word *stressed*. When it comes out (and it always does if you have done your job right), make the point that this is what adults often do to children (of course without meaning to) when asking fact-based questions only. Then, hold up the *Fun and Stress-Free Cue Card* (see page 51) to remind participants to keep reading fun and stress free!

The Cue Card

The *Fun and Stress-Free Cue Card* (see page 51) is an important part of winning over your audience during each session. Once you have introduced it, hold it up a number of times throughout the remainder of this session and during the third session as well. Before long, you will find that your participants will respond to the card quite vocally! It really helps drive home the point and brings your audience into the discussion.

Questioning Strategies

Participants almost always model a fact-based question the first time you try to get them to make up a question for a story you are using to demonstrate the technique. For instance, in *Mary Wore Her Red Dress*, when asking for a model question from a participant, it is not uncommon for the individual to say, "Where is Mary going?" Having shed your "nasty" persona, say "To make that a more friendly question, we might want to ask 'Where do you think Mary is going?'"

Section I

Session 3
Wordless Books and Reader's Theatre

MATERIALS

- Post-it notes

- Big Book stand

- *Fun and Stress-Free Cue Card* (see page 51)

- *The Kiss* (see page 53)
  Three copies of the script (John, Marsha, Narrator)
  John and Marsha signs
  Optional: Props (tie and pearl necklace)

- Recommended books and suggested props (use Big Books if possible; see Appendix B for a complete reference for each book listed):
  Good Dog, Carl
  Good Night, Gorilla
  Tuesday
  Pancakes for Breakfast
  Will's Mammoth
  Clap Your Hands
  From Head to Toe
  Hand Rhymes
  You're Just What I Need
  - Blanket

  Marsupial Sue
  - CD included with *Marsupial Sue* book

  The Very Busy Spider
  - Ball of yarn

Read with Me!

Is Your Mama a Llama?
- Popsicle sticks and *Is Your Mama a Llama? Patterns* (see the accompanying CD-ROM)

There Was an Old Lady Who Swallowed a Fly
- Storytelling apron (see "Reader's Theatre Strategies," page 44)

The Napping House
- Book bag (see "Reader's Theatre Strategies," page 44)

The Very Hungry Caterpillar
- Magazine, paper punch, and glue

- *Using Wordless Books to Increase Thinking Skills* (see page 54)
- *Building Language and Literacy Skills with Reader's Theatre* (see page 55)
- *Joining the Literacy Club* (see page 56)
- *If You Give a Child a Book* (see page 58)
- *Final Project Evaluation* (see page 59)
- *Pre/Post Survey* (see page 45)
- Other wordless books and reader's theatre books to display (see Appendix B)
- Optional (but recommended) items:
  Copies of books for participants
  Self-addressed stamped envelopes (SASEs)
  Refreshments

LESSON PLAN

Opening

1. See "Facilitator's Notes" (page 43) for preparation.
2. Encourage participants to share their experiences at home using last week's strategies. Did they work? Which books did children especially enjoy? Did they find other books that worked well using these strategies?
3. Tell participants that this week two additional strategies will be demonstrated—using wordless books and reader's theatre.
4. Reinforce that reading should be fun and stress free. The goal is not to make children perfect readers—just lovers of literacy. Hold up the *Fun and Stress-Free Cue Card* (see page 51).
5. Perform *The Kiss* (see page 53) with participant volunteers.
6. Have the Big Book stand ready to display books as you talk about them.

Wordless Books

Introduce the Strategy

Talk about how wordless books encourage children to be good thinkers. Explain that wordless books help children discover that what they say can be written and what is written can be read. Point out that wordless books also encourage children to feel like "authors" by letting them make up the words to describe a story that is told through pictures. Emphasize that wordless books allow adults and children freedom to make the story anything they want it to be.

Demonstrate the Strategy with a Specific Book

Use the story *Good Dog, Carl* (or one of the books listed under "Share Additional Books That Support the Strategy") and:

1. Read this entire book (i.e., examine each picture and make appropriate comments) because it so nicely demonstrates the power of wordless books. Also, it usually generates lots of laughter!
2. Model good questioning and predicting strategies as you page through the story. Encourage participants to do the same.

Clarify Proper Use of the Strategy

Remind participants to be sure to ask open-ended questions and provide positive feedback for all verbal responses from the child. They want to make sure reading stays fun and stress free.

Talk about the power and flexibility of using Post-it notes. This technique helps children feel like they are authors. Further, they learn that what can be said can be written and what can be written can be read.

Share Additional Books That Support the Strategy

Share at least two to three additional books to ensure that participants understand the strategy and the kinds of books that support its use. Be sure to demonstrate using open-ended questions and predicting while you are looking through the books. The following books are recommended for practice:

Good Night, Gorilla

1. Ask participants to follow along in their books as you share this story.

Read with Me!

2. As you turn each page, have the person whose book has the Post-it note on that particular page read what he or she wrote. If more than one person was assigned that page, have them both read their ideas.
3. Provide positive feedback to participants (e.g., "Yes, the monkey *is* stealing his keys!")
4. Be sure to model open-ended questions and predicting as you use the book to demonstrate the strategies (e.g., "I wonder whose eyes those are?").

Tuesday

1. Point out the many wonderful pictures that catch children's interest and encourage imaginative responses to open-ended questions.
2. Explain that older children especially like to create their own version of the story line using the Post-it note technique.

Pancakes for Breakfast

Point out that the illustrations do a wonderful job of creating a story that truly grows with the child.

Will's Mammoth

Explain that this book is for children who are a little older or who are more sophisticated readers.

Reader's Theatre

Introduce the Strategy

Discuss how dramatization of stories is a very natural way for children to get really involved in literature. Stress that the point is to help children learn to engage more than just their ears and eyes. Explain that reader's theatre can involve anything from commercial props, to homemade cutouts, to just children themselves. Try to demonstrate all kinds of involvement.

Demonstrate the Strategy with a Specific Book

Explain that with many books, engaging children in reader's theatre involves no props at all. Point out that some stories need only a single prop to help children engage in the story. Demonstrate this by using the story *Clap Your Hands* (or one of the books listed under "Share Additional Books That Support the Strategy," page 41) and:

Have participants respond to commands given in the book.

Clarify Proper Use of the Strategy

Tell participants that the first few times they try reader's theatre techniques, they will probably need to model the behavior they are trying to have children perform. Usually children are very excited about acting out the story. However, explain the importance of not forcing children to participate. Remind participants to keep the focus on the pleasure of enjoying a story with more than just eyes and ears.

Share Additional Books That Support the Strategy

Share at least two to three additional books to ensure that participants understand the strategy and the kinds of books that support its use. Explain that other kinds of books can be acted out with more elaborate props. Many books have commercial props that are available. Consider demonstrating the concept of a "book bag" (see "Reader's Theatre Strategies," page 44) using either commercial props (See Appendix C, *Purchasing Information)* or those you have created yourself. The following books are recommended for practice:

From Head to Toe

Have participants move like the animals in the book and respond "I can do it."

Hand Rhymes

1. Point out that this book has great illustrations for each rhyme, plus a simple picture of hand motions that go along with each line of the rhyme.
2. Demonstrate one of the hand rhymes with the motions ("Here is the Beehive" on page 14 of *Hand Rhymes* is especially good).

You're Just What I Need

1. Explain that this book requires only a blanket and an interested child.
2. Consider reading this entire book. If possible, have someone act out the part of the child using a blanket as a prop. Note that the child adds one more "No!" each time the mother asks a question.

Marsupial Sue

1. Point out that this book has great rhythm and rhyme in a limerick format rather than a more traditional rhyme.
2. Note that the fun part is singing along with the *Marsupial Sue* CD and hopping around like Sue and her friends.

Read with Me!

The Very Busy Spider

1. Explain that acting out this story requires only a ball of yarn.
2. Note that to use reader's theatre for this book, parents and children read the story together using a paired reading strategy.
3. Point out that each time you come to the repetitive phrase ("But the spider didn't answer, she was too busy spinning her web"), the child can loop the yarn around something in the room. Before long, a room-sized spider's web appears!

Is Your Mama a Llama?

1. Explain that this story can be dramatized using simple stick puppets. (See the accompanying CD-ROM for reproducible patterns.)
2. Tell participants to have a child hold up the animal he or she thinks answers each riddle in the story.
3. Explain that all responses should be accepted (e.g., "It could be a bat. Let's see.").

There Was an Old Lady Who Swallowed a Fly

Tell participants to use animals cut from magazines, puppets, or a storytelling apron.

The Napping House

1. Demonstrate this story using both commercial props and homemade props.
2. Consider pointing out the changing light in the illustrations that indicates day and night in the story.

The Very Hungry Caterpillar

1. Show participants how they can make their own book by pasting pictures of foods cut from magazines on paper.
2. Explain that children should dictate the story by naming the foods the caterpillar ate through.
3. Note that a paper punch can be used to make caterpillar holes.

Closing

1. Review information on *Using Wordless Books to Increase Thinking Skills* (see page 54) and *Building Language and Literacy Skills with Reader's Theatre* (see page 55).
2. Introduce participants to the literacy club by discussing the information on the *Joining the Literacy Club* handout (see page 56).
3. Solicit participants suggestions for other books that could support the wordless books and reader's theatre strategies.

4. Finish the session by asking participants to take turns reading the poem *If You Give a Child a Book* (see page 58) stanza by stanza.
5. Have participants complete a *Pre/Post Survey* (see page 45) and/or a *Final Project Evaluation* (see page 59).
6. Optional: Discuss returning the *Pre/Post Survey* (see page 45) and the *Final Project Evaluation* (see page 59). Provide a self-addressed stamped envelope, if possible, to ensure you get feedback from participants.
7. Optional: Invite participants to have some refreshments and look over the books you have on display.

FACILITATOR'S NOTES

Preparation

Before beginning the session, stick one Post-it note on a different page of participants' copies of *Good Night, Gorilla*. (Each book will have one Post-it note and each book will have the Post-it note on a different page.) If you have more participants than pages, it is perfectly acceptable that some books have their Post-it notes on the same pages.

As participants arrive, have them open their copy of the book, find the page with the Post-it note, and write something that they think would represent what is happening on that page.

The Kiss

Prior to the beginning of the session, recruit two "volunteers" to participant in this little skit. It is nice to have a man and a woman—but not absolutely necessary. Provide each with a copy of the script (see page 53) with their lines highlighted.

When the time comes, invite them to the front of the room and put the appropriate "John" or "Marsha" sign around their necks. You may also want to dress John with a tie and Marsha with a string of chunky pearls. With one of the facilitators acting as narrator, perform the play. Use the dialogue of the play as a springboard for discussion regarding how we often make children feel like they are being judged, and they do not even really know what they are doing right or wrong.

If you are working with teachers you do not know, ask another teacher to suggest colleagues who might be good to cast in these parts. If you can find aspiring or closet actors (or just plain hams) the demonstration is lots of fun and makes a strong point.

Reader's Theatre Strategies

You will find many ideas for reader's theatre. Obviously, you can dramatize any number of books in any number of ways. What you want to convey to participants is the idea that there are many different options. Try to provide a mix of simple, inexpensive ideas and more involved dramatization that might even include a few commercial props.

You can find inexpensive book bags (clear bags that hold small props for stories) from a commercial vendor (see Appendix C, *Purchasing Information*). Book bags can also be created by collecting inexpensive trinkets and props from around the house.

You may also want to use storytelling aprons. You can purchase these from commercial vendors, but it is easier to purchase an inexpensive white chef's apron from your local "Dollar" store and add a large pocket, or pockets, to hold small props or felt figures. Sew or glue Velcro strips on the apron in several rows and onto the back of the props you are using. Children can take the figures/props out of the pocket as you read about them and put them on the apron.

Reader's theatre books abound and there are many ways each can be dramatized. Choose your favorites and use your imagination!

Data Collection

If you are asking participants to keep a log of the books they have read and the techniques used, you may wish to provide a SASE for them to be returned by a specified date. In the same way, if you are asking participants to fill out a *Pre/Post Survey* and/or a *Final Project Evaluation,* provide them with a SASE for their convenience.

Pre/Post Survey

How often do you or another adult read to your child?

1 Everyday
2 Almost everyday
3 At least twice a week
4 Once a week
5 Less than once a week

What is your child's current attitude toward being read to?

1 Can't wait to read with you
2 Enjoys reading
3 Will read with you with encouragement
4 Has difficulty sitting still for a story
5 Is not interested

Does your child "read" or "talk" about stories with you or others?

1 Often
2 Sometimes
3 Occasionally
4 Rarely
5 Never

Does your child ask you to read to him or her?

1 Often
2 Sometimes
3 Occasionally
4 Rarely
5 Never

What is your attitude toward reading to your child?

1 Number one priority
2 Can be enjoyable
3 Neutral
4 Really not my thing
5 A chore

How confident are you about your ability to read effectively with your child?

1 Very confident
2 Pretty confident
3 Don't worry about it
4 Not very confident
5 No confidence

How confident are you about picking appropriate books for your child?

1 Very confident
2 Pretty confident
3 Don't worry about it
4 Not very confident
5 No confidence

What do you feel is your role in teaching your child to read?

What is your child's favorite book?

Effective Reading Techniques for Young Readers

1. Allow the child to select some of the books you read.

2. Talk about the different parts of the book, such as front cover, back cover, title, author, beginning, and end.

3. Read slowly (but don't drag it out).

4. Consider allowing the child to hold the book and turn the pages. Show the child how to turn one page at a time.

5. Vary your voice by using lots of intonation and stress.

6. Talk about the story; relate it to the child's experiences.

7. Repeat what the child says; add words to make a full sentence (e.g., CHILD: Truck. ADULT: Yes, that's a big truck!).

8. Monitor the child's face and behavior for signs of boredom or fatigue, and end the session when the child loses interest.

9. Compliment the child on his or her attempts to read. Tell the child that he or she is a reader!

Remember,
make reading together fun and stress free!

How to Include Children in Echo Reading and Paired Reading

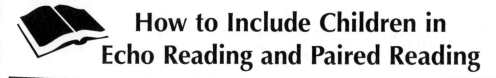

For Echo Reading and Paired Reading:

- Choose books that are predictable and contain simple, repetitive phrases.
- Choose books that have a simple story sequence with one main idea for each page.
- You may need to read a book five times or more before the child feels confident enough to enter into the reading interaction (especially with paired reading).
- Move your finger under the words as you or the child says them.

For Echo Reading:

- You may need to cue the child with phrases such as "Copy me," "Say what I say," or "Now you say it" to help him or her know what to do.
- If the child is not able or not willing to join in, just go on to the next page. Don't force the child to echo.
- Accept all attempts.

For Paired Reading:

- Pause and use voice inflection and facial expressions to signal to the child that it is his or her time to "read."
- Vary the amount of material that the child "reads" according to his or her level. (The child may say only a word or whole pages.)
- If the child is not able or not willing to join in, just read the phrase yourself and keep going. Don't force the child to join in.
- Accept all attempts.

Remember, make reading together fun and stress free!

Reading Log

Date	Book	Strategy(ies)	Time

Name: _____

"Alexander" Quiz

1. Q: What did Alexander find in his breakfast cereal?
   A: Cereal

2. Q: What did Nick find in his cereal box?
   A: Jr. Undercover Agent ring

3. Q: Who had a seat by the window in the car? (3 names)
   A: Becky, Audry, Ellis

4. Q: What number did Alexander forget to count?
   A: 16

5. Q: Who was Paul's best friend?
   A: Phillip Parker

6. Q: What did Albert get in his lunch box?
   A: Hershey bar with almonds

7. Q: Where did Alexander go first after school?
   A: Dentist

8. Q: Where did Alexander go next?
   A: Shoe store

9. Q: What was the third place he went after school?
   A: Dad's office

10. Q: How did this quiz make you feel?

Fun and Stress-Free Cue Card

Suggested Materials: Poster board or foam board
Suggested Size: Ideal size is approximately 24" × 36"
Hint: Make sure you create your cue card so that when you flip it, the other side reads correctly.

Side 1

Side 2

Building Thinking Skills

Asking Questions That Can Help Build Thinking Skills

- Avoid scary questions such as those starting with *who, what, when,* or *where* that have a specific answer.

- Ask friendly questions that have no one "right" answer (open-ended questions).

- Ask questions that develop the child's ability to think beyond the facts given in the story.

- Use phrases such as:

  What do you think...?
  How would you feel if...?
  Who might be..."

- Accept all answers. Give praise for the child's responses.

Helping Children Build Thinking Skills by Making Predictions

- Choose books that have a high-interest level for the child.

- Look for books that give the child an opportunity to make a prediction (such as what might happen next, what might be hidden under the flap, or what a set of clues might be describing).

- Build a new ending by asking the child what might happen next after the last page of the story.

- Do not demand that children's predictions be exact. Children enjoy making silly predictions.

- Accept all answers. Give the child lots of praise for using his or her thinking skills, for example:

What a good idea!
That's a great guess!

Remember,
make reading together fun and stress free!

The Kiss

NARRATOR: John planned a good while, thought carefully about the various ways he might approach the whole business, considered, and reconsidered. But, he wanted to show Marsha how he felt. Finally, he pulled himself together, cast caution aside, and planted his lips firmly on hers. When it was over, John was delighted. He had done it! He was scared, but it was wonderful! Until Marsha said…

MARSHA: John, I could feel your teeth!

JOHN: *[startled]* But, Marsha! I tried my best.

MARSHA: I know, but really John, your breath.

JOHN: What about my breath?

MARSHA: There's something about your breath. You figure it out and be sure it's not the same next time.

JOHN: Oh.

MARSHA: And your eyes. You should close your eyes when you kiss, John.

JOHN: But, Marsha, how would you know if my eyes were open?

MARSHA: I've kissed before, John. I can leave my eyes open if I want to. You can too, later, after you've first learned to close them. Make sure you do it right next time.

JOHN: What do you mean by "right," Marsha?

MARSHA: Doing it without mistakes, John. I'll keep a record of what you did wrong this time. If you avoid doing the wrong things next time, we'll know you're doing it right.

JOHN: Marsha, did you like the kiss?

MARSHA: Whether or not I liked it is not the important thing, John. What matters is whether or not you did it right.

NARRATOR: *[feel free to paraphrase in your own words]* Do you think John will be anxious to kiss Marsha again? Or any girl? If we analyzed every kiss against a specific standard, kissing might be wiped off the face of the earth! Unfortunately, sometimes we make children feel just like John when they trustingly put forth their best attempts at reading and writing. Our job is not to analyze, but to enjoy the experience. Otherwise, children may be reluctant to try again—just like John! So don't be a Marsha!

Using Wordless Books to Increase Thinking Skills

1. Choose books that have a simple, sequential format.

2. Look through the books with the child first, talking about the actions and how the characters might feel.

3. Ask the child to tell you one event that happens on each page as you re-read the book together.

4. Use questioning and predicting strategies to enhance the reading experience.

5. Try using Post-it notes to help the child be the "author." (This helps the child discover that what they say can be written and read again.)

Remember,
make reading together fun
and stress free!

Building Language and Literacy Skills with Reader's Theatre

1. Use the child's natural interest in dramatic play to reenact familiar literature.

2. Choose books that have simple, sequential events.

3. Choose books concerning families, young children, or animals.

4. Gather simple props or provide paper and craft sticks for making puppets to use in dramatization.

5. Be prepared to watch the child's dramatic production over and over and over!

Remember,
make reading together fun and stress free!

Joining the Literacy Club

Most children will learn how to read. Whether they will learn to value the ability and use it effectively to direct their lives depends on their experiences with literacy. Through the use of good literature, effective reading strategies, and a fun and stress-free approach to reading, children can learn to be attracted to reading as a pleasurable experience. Parents who use this approach to literacy can help their children value reading as a desirable alternative to other activities and a tool for becoming a successful person. The following suggestions will help you and your child "join the literacy club" for better language and literacy skills.

Things You Should Do:

- **Talk, talk, talk.** Children who have good language skills and large vocabularies have a better foundation for reading. Discuss everyday and extraordinary events at length. Point out fun things you notice while driving to school. Talk about what you see in the grocery store. Play the I Wonder game (e.g., "I wonder where that fire engine is going?").

- **Read, read, read.** Reading to your child is the single most important literacy building activity that you can provide. Children are never too young or too old to be read to. Choose good books and keep reading fun and stress free.

- **Demonstrate literacy.** To attract children to reading and writing, we must show them what literate adults do. Children must see parents reading, just as they listened to their parents talk, if they are to learn the importance of reading. Newspapers, magazines, and books should literally overflow in a home that is growing a crop of young readers.

- **Support, not correct.** Nobody is as good a reader as they could possibly be. Avoid needlessly correcting children as they read with you. Celebrate their attempts to get things right.

- **Build responsibility.** Provide opportunities for your child to choose his or her own books. Get a library card. Talk about the books your child selected and later talk about whether he or she liked the books.

- **Set reasonable expectations.** Do not expect your child to learn to read overnight, or at the same pace as another child, or to love every book you read. Remember that each child is an individual. We want to encourage reading, not force it.

Things You Do Not Need:

- **Phonic books, phonic tapes, or other workbooks.** Would you want to join a club that was having as much fun as a phonics worksheet? Your child will learn phonics once he or she reaches school age. Better to leave this to the classroom teacher.

- **A critical eye to hunt for errors.** If you are looking for errors, you will surely find them—and that is what your child will focus on. It is more difficult, yet more beneficial, to focus on the successes. Then you become partners in the literacy club!

If You Give a Child a Book

If you give a child a book...
> he will probably ask you to read it.

If you read the book for her...
> she will ask you to read it again and again.

After you have read the book over and over...
> he will ask for some props so he can act it out.

After you have gathered the props for her...
> she will ask you to call her friends so she can put on a play.

After his friends arrive...
> he will ask you to make popcorn and lemonade for his performance.

After the show is over...
> she will ask if her friends can sleep over.

When they are ready for bed...
> he will ask you to read them his favorite story just one more time.

And as you begin to read...
> she will ask if she can read it with you.

AND SHE WILL!

—Helen Davig

Final Project Evaluation

1. I attended the following *Read with Me!* sessions (circle all that apply):

   Session 1   Echo Reading and Paired Reading

   Session 2   Questioning and Predicting

   Session 3   Wordless Books and Reader's Theatre

2. Did attending the workshop(s) change the way that you interacted with your child? How?

3. Do you feel that your attendance at the workshop(s) changed your child's reading behaviors? How?

4. Do you think that you will continue to use these techniques when reading to your child (or to other children). How or why?

5. What aspect(s) of the workshop(s) did you find most beneficial?

6. Do you have any suggestions on how the workshop(s) might be improved?

7. Would you be interested in attending more workshops related to language and reading development?

Section II

Older Children

Read with Me!

CONTENTS

Overview 63
Goals 64
Session 1: Older Children 65
Reading with Older Children 67
Reaching the Reluctant Reader 68

Section II

OVERVIEW

The development of an upper extension to the *Read with Me!* Home program was brought about by continued (and insistent) requests for information regarding how to provide older children with reading experiences based on the *Read with Me!* philosophy and strategies. In addition, parents and teachers who work primarily with older children often asked if the *Read with Me!* program could be used with older children who, for whatever reason, had become reluctant to read. Parents of preschoolers who participate in the Home program quite often have older children in their families as well. Expanding the program to include this group was a natural consequence of the questions often raised at workshops about how to make reading fun and stress free for these children as well.

The *Read with Me!* fundamental philosophy of engaging children in reading through positive literacy experiences is appropriate for any age. With a few modifications and the right books, *Read with Me!* can help children of all ages increase their language and literacy skills.

You may wish to provide participants in a Home program with the opportunity to attend an optional fourth session targeting reading with their older children. This session would generally take place very shortly after the completion of the three Home sessions (usually within a week or two). In this final session, the information is provided through a series of handouts that are reviewed point by point with multiple opportunities for discussion. Because a high level of trust between facilitators and participants is usually well established by this time, this particular session tends to be highly interactive and requires very little prompting by the facilitators. (A specific lesson plan for this scenario is found on page 65.)

Alternatively, if the participants are interested primarily in working with older children (that is, if they have not participated in the Home sessions), a modified workshop may be best. In this instance, the facilitators can present an overview of the *Read with Me!* philosophy using the *Overhead Presentation* provided in Appendix D and short demonstrations of each of six the *Read with Me!* strategies. Following this introduction, the information specifically for working with older children is presented as outlined in the lesson plan on page 65.

As with each variation of the *Read with Me!* program, the information provided in this section can be adapted to suit the needs of individual programs. For instance, although originally designed as a direct training to parents and educators, the handouts in this section can also be sent home as stand-alone suggestions for increasing the fundamental reading skills of children in grades 3–6, and even beyond.

Read with Me!

Note that complete references for all the books mentioned in this section can be found in Appendix B. You may also find it helpful to review "Organization" (see page 18), "Staff Training" (see page 18), "Funding" (see page 18), "Recruitment" (see page 20), "Program Delivery" (see page 20), and "Data Collection" (see page 21) in Section I for information on these topics.

GOALS

- Augment the Home program with strategies for working with children age 8 and older.
- Familiarize participants with individual learning styles to help them better understand why some children learn to read more easily than others.
- Provide participants with information and strategies for working with "reluctant readers."

Section II

Session 1
Older Children

MATERIALS

- *Fun and Stress-Free Cue Card* (see page 51)
- *Reading with Older Children* (see page 67)
- *Reaching the Reluctant Reader* (see page 68)
- Books for demonstration (see Appendix B)
- Optional (but recommended) item: Refreshments

LESSON PLAN

Opening

1. Welcome participants back for another session of fun and stress-free learning. (Consider posting the *Fun and Stress-Free Cue Card* [see page 51] in a conspicuous spot for this session.)
2. If appropriate, ask participants for input regarding how their children enjoyed the previous books and strategies (i.e., reader's theatre and wordless books).
3. Emphasize that older readers also need quality reading interactions, both by being read to and by reading on their own. However, some special considerations are necessary when working with this age group.

Introduce

1. Talk about how the *Read with Me!* strategies that are used with preschoolers are still appropriate for older children; you just apply them to different books.
2. Go over the *Reading with Older Children* handout (see page 67) point by point, discussing each major and minor point.
3. Encourage participants to share their experiences about reading with their older children as well as to ask questions and provide examples related to the handout.

Read with Me!

Expand

1. Review the *Reaching the Reluctant Reader* (see page 68) handout. Talk about each major and minor point.
2. Emphasis that the most important thing is to get the child to read anything!
3. Discuss the importance of considering each child's learning style and interests when selecting books.
4. Emphasize that adults should make an effort to praise children's reading attempts and successes. Criticism is not a useful construct, especially with reluctant readers.

Demonstrate

1. Share books with participants as you go through the appropriate sections of Appendix B.
2. Try to have a number of books for participants to browse at this more informal session.
3. Encourage participants to share books that they have in their collections that fit the categories.

Summarize

1. Remind participants that reading with school-age children is just as important as reading with preschoolers.
2. Emphasize the importance of keeping reading pleasurable. Remind participants not to force children to read beyond their abilities. (This is a good place to use the *Fun and Stress-Free Cue Card* one last time.)
3. Encourage participants to share what they have learned with others.

Closing

1. Thank participants for attending and for their continued interest in helping their children become the best readers they can be.
2. Encourage participants to keep in touch with one another (and with you) to share books and experiences.
3. Optional: Offer refreshments and provide time for book browsing and socializing.

 # Reading with Older Children

Don't stop reading aloud to your child just because he or she has moved beyond second grade.

- Note that children continue to benefit from parent-child reading interactions well into the middle school years.
- Pick books that include humor, lots of action sequences, and interesting characters (e.g., *Hank the Cowdog* series).
- Don't be afraid to read books without pictures—let children use their imaginations.
- Continue shared reading experiences, especially with reluctant/slow readers (this promotes increases in vocabulary, grammar, story construction, and comprehension).
- Take time to say aloud what you are thinking about the story.

Don't be afraid to read books of ANY level to your child.

- Revisit "old friends" in your child's favorite books.
- Let your child repeat successful reading experiences often!

Make reading together a part of your daily routine.

- Take turns reading to one another.
- Take turns reading together to a younger sibling. Have the older child use *Read with Me!* strategies.
- Pass your child the comics section of the newspaper on Sunday mornings.
- Read on car trips. Choose books that have great characters and lots of action. Choose books your child may not be able to read independently, but will enjoy. Choose books about where you might be going.
- Consider books on tape (check them out at the library). Make your own books on tape!
- Get a library card. Keep a special basket for library books in a cozy spot. And don't forget to get some books for yourself too!

Remember, make reading together fun and stress free!

Reaching the Reluctant Reader

Reading anything is better than reading nothing.

- Don't pressure reluctant readers to read books that they are not interested in.
- Provide children with many alternatives for engaging in literacy experiences (e.g., comic books, magazines, and closed caption television).

Consider your child's strengths, interests, and preferred learning styles.

- Use books that are rich in visual detail rather than in literary detail for visual learners (they enjoy pictures rather than words).
- Choose books with topics that hold special interest to children, such as sports, horses, magic, and dinosaurs.

Tickle your child's funny bone.

- Don't suppress silliness. Children's love for silliness does not just die—adults kill it!
- Explore books that are filled with unexpected story lines, puns, funny pictures, and general humor.

Don't be afraid to let your child read comic books!

- Take turns reading them together. Predict new endings. Extend the story by drawing your own version of the comic.
- Use anthologies—they provide children with multiple opportunities to read small amounts at a time within the constructs of a large volume (seems more like a "real" book).

Continue to model reading behaviors and include your child in the activity.

- Ask your child to recommend a book and then read it.
- Ask your child to help you select a book as a gift for someone else.
- Reward children with time reading together instead of trinkets and toys.
- Let your child choose books from school book clubs.

Section III

School

Read with Me!

CONTENTS

Overview	71
Goals	72
Organization	72
Staff Training	72
Funding	73
Recruitment	73
Program Delivery	74
Poetry and Chapter Books	75
Data Collection	76
Book Knowledge Assessment	78
Video Script 1: *I Went Walking*	80
Video Script 2: *The Secret Birthday Message*	81
Video Script 3: *Is Your Mama a Llama?*	82
Video Script 4: *Deep in the Forest*	83
Video Script 5: *The Doorbell Rang*	84
Reading Suggestions Labels	85
Alternate Reading Suggestions Labels	87
Facilitator Duties	89
Sample Weekly Meeting Agenda	91
Facilitator Observations	92
Sample Observation Comments	93
Parent Permission Letter	95
Parent Conference Letter	96
Read with Me! Brochure	97
Student Interest Survey	99
Daily Facilitator Log	100
Take-Home Book List	101
Parent Video Evaluation: Echo Reading	102
Parent Video Evaluation: Paired Reading	103
Parent Video Evaluation: Questioning and Predicting	104
Parent Video Evaluation: Wordless Books	105
Parent Video Evaluation: Reader's Theatre	106
Read with Me! Success Report	107
Read with Me! Success Report (Sample)	108
Read with Me! Success Award	109
Student Achievement Checklist	110

OVERVIEW

The School program was developed to provide selected students with successful reading experiences and to build their self-confidence as readers. Because many children who have language and communication delays experience related delays in reading, the School program can be especially beneficial in helping build skills in both domains. It is also an effective method of helping parents become more aware of what they can do to support their children in achieving reading and language goals.

Results from a five-year study in the School District of Holmen, WI, of the School program (titled "Reading Together in Kindergarten") indicated that emergent readers increased understanding of concepts of print, awareness of words and letters, beginning development of letter-sound relationships, beginning awareness of story structure, and beginning awareness of stability of print. Transitional readers increased voice/print matching, usage of pictures to help develop some sight word and letter recognition, development of decoding strategies, retelling stories with some detail, and knowledge of letters and their corresponding sounds. Further, 72% of preschool students who participated in the School program's reading sessions scored above the at-risk level when given the *Book Knowledge Assessment* (see pages 78–79) in kindergarten. Parents who participated through the videotaped sessions increased the amount of interactive reading strategies used during home reading and applied these strategies to other books. Parents also related that their children demonstrated a greater interest in, and enthusiasm for, reading books.

Teachers, teaching assistants, or volunteers who have been trained in the use of the six *Read with Me!* strategies (see *"Read with Me!* Strategies," page 10) and in the Home workshops are the facilitators (these facilitators are supervised by the program coordinator). The School program facilitators conduct one-to-one, 15-minute sessions each day with qualified students. (Qualified students are identified by scoring seven or less on the *Book Knowledge Assessment* [see pages 78–79] and/or through teacher referrals.)

To provide a bridge between home and school, demonstrations of each reading strategy are videotaped and sent home with each child throughout the year. After a child becomes proficient in using a specific strategy, he or she is videotaped reading a book with his or her School program facilitator that demonstrates that strategy. During the videotaped session, the facilitator describes for the parents what strategy is being used and how the strategy can help children build language skills. Suggestions for language extension activities that can be implemented at home are also provided on videos (see pages 80–84). These strategies encourage parents to become active participants in the School program and to take ownership in helping their child learn. Eventually, most parents realize that they can make a significant difference in their child's school success.

Read with Me!

Please note, *Read with Me!* programs are very compatible, so parents could elect to participate in Home workshops (if available) while their children are receiving direct tutoring through the School program. However, it is certainly not a requirement. Again, *Read with Me!* can be tailored to any setting at the discretion of the program coordinator.

GOALS

- Provide successful early literacy experiences to preschool and kindergarten students (i.e., ages 3–7).
- Build children's self-confidence as readers.
- Introduce children and parents to a variety of children's literature.
- Involve parents through videotapes of their child's reading sessions.
- Facilitate home language experiences by helping parents learn to apply the School program's strategies to other books.

ORGANIZATION

In preparation for the School program, complete the following tasks:

1. Obtain a 14-gallon plastic container with a cover (e.g., a Rubbermaid Tote) for each facilitator's set of books.
2. Use colored file folder dividers to separate the books in each container into reading strategy categories (e.g., echo reading = red and paired reading = blue).
3. Use colored stickers that match the colored dividers to color-code each book by reading strategy category.
4. Make *Reading Suggestions Labels* (see pages 85–86 and 87–88) and place them in selected take-home books.

STAFF TRAINING

Facilitators should receive one six-hour training session (or three two-hour sessions) on how to implement the *Read with Me!* interactive reading strategies. Facilitators generally work part time, serving 12 children a day. A detailed list of duties for School program facilitators is provided (see pages 89–90).

When School program implementation includes a team of facilitators, it may be helpful to conduct biweekly facilitator meetings. This gives facilitators an opportunity to share successes

Section III

and challenges, discuss adaptations, and collect data (see *Sample Weekly Meeting Agenda*, page 91). You may want to keep a record of a few students' progress and share these comments at the meetings. (See *Facilitator Observations* and *Sample Observation Comments*, pages 92–94).

FUNDING

Required resources and approximate costs associated with the implementation of a School program to serve 48 children are detailed in Figure 3.1. If you are implementing the program on a smaller scale, costs will be reduced proportionally.

Figure 3.1 — **Sample Start-Up Budget**

Staff costs (four half-time teaching assistants or two teaching assistants and two volunteers) ....Market cost

Set of take-home books (6 paperback books × 48 children = 288 books × $4 per book = $1,152) and *Reading Suggestions Labels* (6 labels each for 48 children × $1 per label set (6) = $48) $1,200

48 videotapes ($2 each) $96

4 facilitator book sets (10 books per strategy × 6 strategies = 60 books × $6 per book = $360 × 4 facilitators = $1,440), totes/tubs ($10 each × 4 facilitators = $40), colored file folder dividers ($1.25 per set [6] × 4 sets = $5), and 288 colored stickers ($5) $1,490

TOTAL ....$2,786 (+ staff costs)

($58.04 average per child, plus staff costs)

RECRUITMENT

One of the key components to the success of a School program is consistent daily tutoring sessions. If volunteers are to be used to implement this program, they must be able to commit to steady attendance. Sources for recruiting volunteer facilitators include local AmeriCorp chapters, retired teacher organizations, Rotary Clubs and other service organizations, high school student volunteer groups, and your school's parent/teacher meetings. Of course, if you are doing the tutoring yourself, recruiting is not an issue.

Read with Me!

PROGRAM DELIVERY

The size of the program (in terms of how many children are served) is entirely up to the program coordinator. Again, the program can be adapted to meet the needs of the students and the setting. However, as a general guideline, the following tasks should be completed:

1. Facilitators send home the *Parent Permission Letter* (see page 95) with each student participating in the program along with a brochure describing the School program (see pages 97–98).
2. Facilitators complete facilitator training (if unfamiliar with the *Read with Me!* strategies).
3. Facilitators organize book tubs (see "Organization," page 72).
4. Facilitators assist preschool or kindergarten teachers with giving the *Book Knowledge Assessment* (see pages 78–79) to all students, or they personally give the assessment to targeted students. All students scoring seven or below qualify for the program.
5. Facilitators develop a schedule in which each qualified student receives a 15-minute, individual session every day.
6. On day two or three, facilitators complete the *Student Interest Survey* (see page 99) with each student.
7. Facilitators develop individual sessions with echo reading and progress through each of the *Read with Me!* strategies according to the individual student's interest and ability levels.
8. Facilitators keep a daily log that indicates books read and each student's response (see page 100).
9. If the school has fall parent-teacher conferences, facilitators send the *Parent Conference Letter* (see page 96) home.
10. After one month, facilitators complete the *Student Achievement Checklist* (see page 110).
11. In November, January, February, March, and April, facilitators make a videotape of each student and his or her facilitator demonstrating a reading strategy. (See pages 80–84 for video scripts.)
12. After completing each video demonstration, each student takes home his or her demonstration video, a paperback copy of the book demonstrated (see *Take-Home Book List*, page 101), and a *Parent Video Evaluation* form (see pages 102–106). Placed on the inside cover of the book is a label that has specific reading suggestions for the parent to use while reading the book (see *Reading Suggestions Labels*, pages 85–86).
13. To encourage continued reading interactions within the home, families are encouraged to keep the book; however, the videotape is returned to school with the student so that additional demonstrations can be recorded (This is the best method. However, if funding is tight, you may ask parents to return the book with the videotape.) Parents

Section III

are encouraged to respond to the videotape by completing the *Parent Video Evaluation* form (see pages 102–106) and returning it along with the videotape within one week.

14. At the end of the school year, facilitators allow students to keep their own videotapes. As the sessions are taped consecutively, the videotape provides a treasured keepsake for parents.
15. Facilitators communicate regularly with the student's classroom teacher regarding the his or her progress and any concerns facilitators may have.
16. Facilitators also communicate with parents regularly. Twice a year, facilitators complete a Read with Me! *Success Report* (see page 107 for a blank form and page 108 for a sample completed form). This is shared with parents and teachers during a scheduled meeting time at both fall and spring school parent/teacher conferences.
17. At the end of the year, facilitators give each student a Read With Me! *Success Award* (see page 109).

School program facilitators need to care about young children, enjoy reading, and be willing to share their excitement for books with children. School program sessions are most effective if facilitators (regardless of whether they are professional educators or volunteers) keep the following tips in mind:

- Find a quiet location in the school where the facilitator and the student can be uninterrupted during reading sessions.
- Conduct the School program sessions in an informal, non-threatening environment that promotes an enjoyment of and appreciation for literacy.
- Keep reading sessions fun and stress free!
- Gently encourage verbal participation by students and praise any effort abundantly.
- Add creative hands-on activities for reading extension if desired.
- Discover students' individual interests and find additional books in school or local community libraries. (See Appendix B for the *Expanded Book List*.)

POETRY AND CHAPTER BOOKS

Poetry and chapter books, which are not generally taught in the Home program, are included in this program. Good children's poetry books capture a young student's interests and reflect events from their daily life. The musical lure of the words helps build awareness of phonemic sounds and rhyme. Chapter books give students the opportunity to develop listening skills, stimulate their imaginations, and increase attention span. The best young children's chapter books include humor, action, and lots of dialogue. By the second semester of kindergarten, students are eager to hear the adventures in chapter books for young readers, such as *Dinosaurs Before Dark* (Magic Treehouse Series) and the *Arthur* series. These books, along with other recommended poetry and chapter books, are listed in Appendix B.

While reading poetry and chapter books during School program sessions remember to:

- Choose humorous, action-filled books about young children or animals.
- Read only as long as the student remains interested. Five to ten minutes may be enough for a young listener.
- Read frequently from books without pictures to stimulate imagination.
- Although a videotape is not made of chapter book reading, be sure to give a chapter book as the student's last School program take-home book.

DATA COLLECTION

It is always good practice to keep detailed records and gather data regarding the participation and progress of the children involved in the program. To facilitate this, the following resources are provided:

- *Daily Facilitator Log* sheets (see page 100) record books read and student responses.

- *Book Knowledge Assessment* forms (see pages 78–79) document growth in basic book knowledge. Program eligibility (a score of seven or below) is determined by the pre-assessments given in September or upon entrance to the program. Academic growth is documented by administering the post-assessment at the end of the school year or upon program dismissal or withdrawal.

- *Student Interest Survey* forms (see page 99) indicate increased interest, parent participation, and self-concept as a reader when used periodically. Administer a pre-survey during the first week of program sessions. Post-surveys are administered at the end of the school year or upon dismissal or withdrawal from the program.

- *Student Achievement Checklist* forms (see page 110) indicate emergent reading skills. Pre-checklists are completed during the first week of program sessions. Post-checklists are completed at the end of the school year or upon dismissal or withdrawal from the program.

- *Parent Video Evaluation* forms (see pages 102–106) track parent involvement. Special attention is given to the number of parents using the strategies and extension activities with other books.

Long-term follow-up through compilation of second and third grade test scores for past School program students is highly recommended.

Book Knowledge Assessment

Child: _____ Date: _____ Score: _____/12

Teacher: _____ Building: _____ Qualifies: YES   NO
                                                  (7 or fewer checks = YES)

Teacher Recommendation:

Do you agree with the assessment score?   YES   NO
(If NO, please explain on back.)

1. Using the book *Ice Cream*, ask the student the following questions. Check each correctly completed task. Leave blank tasks that are not completed or are completed incorrectly.

   _____ Can you show me the front cover of the book?

   _____ Can you show me the back cover of the book?

   _____ Can you show me where I will start reading the story?

   _____ Can you show me a letter in the book?

   _____ Can you show me a word in the book?

2. Begin reading *Ice Cream*. After the first five pages, tell the student that you want him or her to finish the story. Observe the student's oral language as well as the way the student turns the book pages. Check each item that applies; leave blank those that do not.

   _____ Child appears interested.

_____ Child knows how to handle a book.

_____ Child responds to questions like "What do you think will happen here?" and "What do you think will happen next?"

_____ Child uses complete sentences during book discussion.

_____ Child uses phrases during book discussion.

_____ Child uses words during book discussion.

_____ Child uses discussion points that are relevant to the story.

From *Reading Together in Kindergarten Handbook* (p. 18) by Helen Davig and Cynthia Jacobson, Instructional Services Department, 1998, Holmen, WI: Holmen School District. © 1998 by the Holmen School District. Adapted with permission.

Video Script 1
I Went Walking

FACILITATOR:

1. Hi, my name is *[state name here]*.

2. This is the first videotape and book packet that your child will be bringing home. The book is for your child to keep. We hope you enjoy watching this video that demonstrates how to echo read a story with your child.

3. When echo reading, you will read a short phrase and then ask your child to repeat what you read by using prompts like "Copy me" or "Say what I say." While using echo reading, point to each word as it is read.

4. Today *[state child's name]* and I are going to read *I Went Walking* together. We are going to do this by echo reading each page. I will read the page and then pause and wait for *[state child's name]* to say the words after me.

5. Echo reading is a fun way to get your child involved with reading a book. When you read this book with your child, read slowly so he or she can easily remember the words. Help your child notice the words by drawing your finger under the words as you read them.

6. *[Demonstrate how to interest the child in a story by talking about the cover picture and title. Just do this without reference to what you are doing or why—you will talk about this next month.]*

7. *[Echo read* I Went Walking, *pausing to let the child repeat each page. Stop and talk about what might be coming next in the story before turning the page.]*

8. *[Show the Reading Suggestions Label placed inside the book.]* Doing extra fun activities with books helps to make literature a part of your child's everyday life. A fun reading suggestion given inside the book cover is to take a walk with your child around the neighborhood or inside your house. Try echo chanting the book's words "I Went Walking…What Did You See?" Put in the words of an object you see on your walk, such as "I saw an oak tree looking at me."

9. Thank you for letting us share our *Read with Me!* session with you. *[State child's name]* can keep this copy of *I Went Walking*. Please return the videotape and *Parent Video Evaluation* to your child's teacher by *[state when to return]*.

From *Reading Together in Kindergarten Handbook* (p. 39) by Helen Davig and Cynthia Jacobson, Instructional Services Department, 1998, Holmen, WI: Holmen School District. © 1998 by the Holmen School District. Adapted with permission.

Video Script 2
The Secret Birthday Message

FACILITATOR:

1. Hi, my name is *[state name here]*.

2. Today *[state child's name]* and I are going to read *The Secret Birthday Message* together. Reading together helps to build a child's confidence in his or her ability to learn to read and is a fun activity for both reader and child.

3. When pair reading, you will read part of a phrase, book, or story and your child then takes a turn and reads another part. You can use pausing, intonation, and stress to signal your child when it is his or her turn to read.

4. *[Talk to the parents about how to draw the child's attention to the story by discussing the cover picture, title, and author. Explain that the cover picture and title hint at what the story is about. Also, the author usually has a familiar "voice" from book to book, and you want the child to start recognizing authors they prefer.]*

5. *[Talk to the parents about what you will be doing to encourage the child to read with you (e.g., pausing before familiar words and running your finger under the words as you read).]*

6. *[Begin reading the book. Start by demonstrating how to focus the child's attention on the book.]*

7. *[Show the secret birthday message part to the camera.]*

8. *[Ask the child to help you read the secret words by guessing what the pictures might be.]*

9. *[Continue reading, asking the child to turn the pages as you read.]*

10. *[Ask the child to follow the map at the end of the book and tell about the boy's search in the story.]*

11. Reading together with your child is fun, and it is an important way to build your child's interest in books. *[State child's name]* can keep this copy of *The Secret Birthday Message*.

12. *[Show the* Reading Suggestions Label *placed inside the book.]* Inside the book cover are more reading suggestions for you to do together. You and your child might want to try this reading style with other favorite books from your home or library.

13. Thanks for letting us share our *Read with Me!* session with you. I hope you enjoyed watching this tape. Please return it and the *Parent Video Evaluation* to your child's teacher by *[state when to return]*.

From *Reading Together in Kindergarten Handbook* (p. 40) by Helen Davig and Cynthia Jacobson, Instructional Services Department, 1998, Holmen, WI: Holmen School District. © 1998 by the Holmen School District. Adapted with permission.

Video Script 3
Is Your Mama a Llama?

FACILITATOR:

1. Hi. Today *[state child's name]* and I are going to read *Is Your Mama a Llama?* While we read this book, I am going to ask *[state child's name]* to use picture and word clues to guess what comes next in the story.

2. Talking about a story as you read it is important. Asking friendly questions is an easy way to involve your child with the story. Guessing what comes next can be fun. Find something positive to say about all your child's guesses and you will help your child become a confident reader.

3. *[Demonstrate how to put picture and word clues together by reading* Is Your Mama a Llama? *Pause and let the child guess what comes next, reinforcing his or her answers with positive comments.]*

4. *[Show the* Reading Suggestions Label *placed inside the book.]* The reading suggestions given inside this book can also be used for other books in your home. Use the tool of asking friendly questions as a way to involve your child with other stories.

5. Thank you for letting us share our *Read with Me!* session with you. *[State child's name]* can keep this copy of *Is Your Mama a Llama?* Please return the videotape and the *Parent Video Evaluation* to your child's teacher by *[state when to return]*.

From *Reading Together in Kindergarten Handbook* (p. 41) by Helen Davig and Cynthia Jacobson, Instructional Services Department, 1998, Holmen, WI: Holmen School District. © 1998 by the Holmen School District. Adapted with permission.

Video Script 4
Deep in the Forest

FACILITATOR:

1. Hi. Today *[state child's name]* and I are going to read the wordless book *Deep in the Forest*. Wordless books give children the chance to make up their own words to a story. When children's words are written down and then read back to them, children start to make the connection that words can be said, written, and read.

2. I started out by telling the story to *[state child's name]*. Telling a wordless book is easier if you don't try to tell everything that is happening on each page. Just pick one idea to talk about and then go on to the next page.

3. I am going to ask *[state child's name]* to tell me the story. As he or she talks, I am going to write the exact words on Post-it notes. They stick easily to each page and do not hurt the book. When *[state child's name]* is finished telling the story, I will go back and read his or her story.

4. *[Demonstrate wordless books. Have the child tell the story as you write on the Post-it notes. Then go back and read the child's story.]*

5. Reading wordless books is a fun way for your child to be involved with literature by becoming an author of his or her own stories. Other wordless books may be found in your school library or your local public library and bookstores.

6. *[Show the* Reading Suggestions Label *placed inside the book.]* The reading suggestions placed on the label inside the book will help remind you to read through the story first, and then ask your child to retell one event that happens on each page as you reread the book together

7. Thank you for letting us share our *Read with Me!* session with you. *[State child's name]* can keep this copy of *Deep in the Forest*. Please return the videotape and the *Parent Video Evaluation* to your child's teacher by *[state when to return]*.

From *Reading Together in Kindergarten Handbook* (p. 42) by Helen Davig and Cynthia Jacobson, Instructional Services Department, 1998, Holmen, WI: Holmen School District. © 1998 by the Holmen School District. Adapted with permission.

Video Script 5
The Doorbell Rang

FACILITATOR:

1. Hi. *[State child's name]* and I are going to read the book *The Doorbell Rang*. Since children love to retell and act out their favorite stories, today we have gathered some simple props to help us act out the story as we read it.

2. For the book *The Doorbell Rang,* we will need a dozen real or pretend cookies, a serving plate, and a bell.

3. As we read through the story, I am going to ask *[state child's name]* to help me read by saying the repeated phrase "No one makes cookies like Grandma!"

4. *[Demonstrate acting out the story as you read* The Doorbell Rang. *Pause before the repeated phrase "No one makes cookies like Grandma" to encourage the child to join in with you.]*

5. Providing the props for children to act out stories at home is fun and easy to do. You do not need fancy props or elaborate costumes. By encouraging your child to act out stories during play time, you will help make literature a part of your child's daily life.

6. *[Show the Reading Suggestions Label placed inside the book.]* These suggestions will remind you how you can make literacy a part of your child's everyday life through acting out stories.

7. Thank you for letting us share our *Read with Me!* session with you. *[State child's name]* can keep this copy of *The Doorbell Rang*. Please return the videotape and *Parent Video Evaluation* to your child's teacher by *[state when to return]*.

From *Reading Together in Kindergarten Handbook* (p. 43) by Helen Davig and Cynthia Jacobson, Instructional Services Department, 1998, Holmen, WI: Holmen School District. © 1998 by the Holmen School District. Adapted with permission.

Reading Suggestions Labels

I Went Walking
- Let your child hold the book.
- Read slowly.
- Echo read this book with your child.
- Take a walk around your yard or nearby park, saying the echo chant, "I went walking. What did you see? I saw a big tree looking at me."
- Echo read another book from your home or library.

The Secret Birthday Message
- Read the secret message note. Let your child guess what each black shape might be.
- Read the story, encouraging your child to look at the picture clues. Pause before each "shape" word. Let your child say it.
- Move your finger under each sentence as you read.
- Help your child write his or her own "secret message" by using picture clues.
- Encourage your child to say familiar words with you while reading other books.

Is Your Mama a Llama?
- Involve your child in the story by stopping to ask what might happen next.
- Don't demand that children's predictions be "right." Children enjoy making silly predictions.
- Find something to praise about your child's prediction.
- Pause and let your child make predictions while reading other books.

Deep in the Forest
- "Read" through the book with your child first, talking about the actions of the story.
- Ask your child to tell you one event that happens on each page as you reread the book together.
- Use Post-it notes to write your child's exact words for each page.
- Reread your child's words and he or she will discover that what one says can be written and read again.
- Look for wordless books at the library, and read them with your child.

The Doorbell Rang

- Read this story several times, as often as your child asks.
- Ask your child to join in with the reading by saying the repeated phrase "No one makes cookies like Grandma!"
- Make or buy cookies and ask your child to gather simple props for acting out the story.
- Have fun acting out the story together.
- Act out the story with your child.

Dinosaurs Before Dark

- Find a quiet time of day to read short segments of the chapter book to your child. Read a little every day.
- Encourage your child to listen by stopping to talk about the story as you read.
- Stop reading when your child begins to lose interest.
- When you begin the following day, make a short comment about what you read the day before.
- Find another *Magic Tree House* series book at the library, and read it with your child.

From *Reading Together in Kindergarten Handbook* (pp. 15–16) by Helen Davig and Cynthia Jacobson, Instructional Services Department, 1998, Holmen, WI: Holmen School District. © 1998 by the Holmen School District. Adapted with permission.

Alternate Reading Suggestions Labels

Down by the Bay
- Let your child hold the book.
- Read slowly.
- Echo read this book with your child.
- Continue echo reading each phrase throughout the book.
- Try echo chanting or singing the book too!
- Echo read another book from your home or library.

Mortimer
- Encourage your child to read along with you.
- Read the story, moving your finger under the repeated phrases in the story.
- Pause before you get to phrases and encourage your child to say them with you.
- Ask your child to sing or say the "Clang, Clang" chant with you.
- Encourage your child to say familiar words with you while reading other books.

There's a Nightmare in My Closet
- Involve your child in the story by stopping to ask what might happen next.
- Don't demand that children's predictions be "right." Children enjoy making silly predictions.
- Find something to praise about your child's prediction.
- Pause and let your child make predictions while reading other books.

Frog, Where Are You?
- "Read" through the book with your child first, talking about the actions of the story.
- Ask your child to tell you one event that happens on each page as you reread the book together.
- Use Post-it notes to write your child's exact words for each page.
- Reread your child's words and he or she will discover that what one says can be written and read again.
- Look for wordless books at the library, and read them with your child.

City Storm

- Read this story several times, as often as your child asks.
- Help your child gather simple props, or make stick puppets to use in acting.
- Use your child's natural interests in play to act out the story.
- Be prepared to watch your child's dramatic production over and over!
- Act out other stories with your child.

Alternate Title from the Magic Tree House Series

- Find a quiet time of day to read short segments of the chapter book to your child. Read a little every day.
- Encourage your child to listen by stopping to talk about the story as you read.
- Stop reading when your child begins to lose interest.
- When you begin the following day, make a short comment about what you read the day before.
- Find another *Magic Tree House* series book at the library, and read it with your child.

From *Reading Together in Kindergarten Handbook* (pp. 16–17) by Helen Davig and Cynthia Jacobson, Instructional Services Department, 1998, Holmen, WI: Holmen School District. © 1998 by the Holmen School District. Adapted with permission.

Facilitator Duties

September

- Participate in *Read with Me!* training.
- Introduce yourself to kindergarten teachers.
- Organize books and record-keeping materials.
- Assist kindergarten teachers with assessing students using the *Book Knowledge Assessment* form (see pages 78–79).
- Ask a kindergarten teacher to introduce you at a staff meeting.
- Search for additional books in libraries.
- Send the *Parent Permission Letter* (see page 95) home to parents.
- Set up a *Read with Me!* student session schedule.

October
(First Week with Children)

- Attend biweekly *Read with Me!* facilitator meetings with the Title I coordinator (continue throughout year).
- Begin student sessions using the echo reading strategy.
- Administer the *Student Interest Survey* (see page 99).
- Start record keeping.
- Schedule parent contacts to coincide with school district conferences.
- Complete the pre *Student Achievement Checklist* (see page 110).

November

- Videotape each student demonstrating the echo reading strategy for parents.
- Send home echo reading videotape, echo reading take-home book, and *Parent Video Evaluation* (see page 102).
- Prepare the Read with Me! *Success Report* (see page 107) for conferences.
- Meet parents at scheduled time during parent/teacher conferences
- Keep records of parent conferences.
- Share Read with Me! *Success Report* with kindergarten teacher.

December

- Introduce paired reading into student sessions.
- Turn in completed list of parent contacts and notes to program coordinator.

January

- Videotape each student demonstrating the paired reading strategy for parents.
- Send home paired reading videotape, paired reading take-home book, and *Parent Video Evaluation* (see page 103).
- Introduce questioning and predicting strategies into student sessions.

February

- Videotape each student demonstrating questioning and predicting strategies for parents.
- Send home questioning and predicting videotape, take-home book, and *Parent Video Evaluation* (see page 104).
- Introduce wordless books into student sessions.

March

- Videotape each student demonstrating wordless book strategies for parents.
- Send home wordless book videotape, take-home book, and *Parent Video Evaluation* (see page 105).
- Schedule parent contacts for spring parent/teacher conferences
- Prepare Read with Me! *Success Report* (see page 107) for conferences.
- Meet parents at scheduled time during parent-teacher conferences
- Keep records of parent conferences.
- Share Read with Me! *Success Report* with kindergarten teacher.
- Introduce reader's theatre into student sessions.

April

- Videotape each student demonstrating reader's theatre strategy for parents.
- Send home reader's theatre videotape, take-home book, and *Parent Video Evaluation* (see page 106).
- Turn in completed list of parent contacts and notes to program coordinator.
- Introduce poetry and chapter books into student sessions.

May

- Send home chapter book take-home book.
- Administer the *Book Knowledge Assessment* (see pages 78–79).
- Administer the *Student Interest Survey* (see page 99).
- Send home the Read With Me! *Success Award* (see page 109).
- Complete the post *Student Achievement Checklist* (see page 110).

From *Reading Together in Kindergarten Handbook* (p. 9) by Helen Davig and Cynthia Jacobson, Instructional Services Department, 1998, Holmen, WI: Holmen School District. © 1998 by the Holmen School District. Adapted with permission.

Sample Weekly Meeting Agenda

Observations about the *Read With Me!* students and program.

I. Successes
   _____
   _____

II. Challenges
   _____
   _____

III. Adjustments
   _____
   _____
   _____

IV. Videotape Update

V. End of Year Deadlines: Handout

VI. Brochure Update

VII. Schedule for Visitors April 29: Handout

VIII. Possible Additions to Core Collections: What Strategy Do They Fit? April 29

IX. Review Revised Parent Survey

X. Next Meeting: April 29

From *Reading Together in Kindergarten Handbook* (p. 11) by Helen Davig and Cynthia Jacobson, Instructional Services Department, 1998, Holmen, WI: Holmen School District. © 1998 by the Holmen School District. Adapted with permission.

Facilitator Observations

Facilitators may choose to keep observation notes on a few selected students. Notes need not be done weekly, but as facilitators observe changes in reading readiness or behavior. These may be compiled at the end of the year to give a record of progress.

_____   _____
Facilitator   Date

_____   _____
Student   Date

_____   _____
Student   Date

From *Reading Together in Kindergarten Handbook* (p. 12) by Helen Davig and Cynthia Jacobson, Instructional Services Department, 1998, Holmen, WI: Holmen School District. © 1998 by the Holmen School District. Adapted with permission.

Sample Observation Comments

Here are some examples of the kinds of observations that could go on the *Facilitator Observations* form (see page 92).

October 4
His teacher suggested that this child might be difficult to work with. His father told the teacher that he had never finished school and that as soon as he could, he would let his son quit school like he did. He indicated that the child was not interested in reading books at home. The child started the *Read with Me!* program with a negative attitude—not interested at all in books or reading.

November 18
The child is continually in a rush to finish books. He uses an angry tone when talking and frequently scowls.

December 4
Though the child often "gets in trouble" in his classroom, he now goes willingly to *Read with Me!* sessions. However, up to this time, the AmeriCorps member had never seen him smile. During the first week in December she saw him smile for the first time.

January 16
The child had been extremely hesitant to participate verbally with book reading. But today he finally took a chance and joined in on the repetitive phrase "jump, frog, jump." He was so proud that he wanted to read the book two more times.

February 26
He is now becoming more animated and interested in stories. He particularly likes the book *The Eyes of Gray Wolf*. He is often laughing and smiling and has begun to ask questions and interact with the stories.

March 14
While in the school hallway, he came up to the AmeriCorps member, gave her a big hug, and then ran away! During the *Read with Me!* session, he began pointing to the repeated phrase, "Oh Mama" in the book *Oh Mama* as they read it together.

April 15
He told the AmeriCorps member that he reads the *Read with Me!* books she sent home with him every day. He now begs to be able to take more books home to read. His parents' attitude about their child's participation in the Title I *Read with Me!* program has changed. They are more positive about their child's involvement, reported his kindergarten teacher.

April 18

He is still very excited about getting books to keep. Asks, "When can I get another one?" He told the AmeriCorps member, "I have the other books you gave me right up on my dresser. And my mom says she's going to get a special box to put them in."

April 25

He is now bringing in books from home and asking the AmeriCorps member to read them to him. He brought in *Lassie* and asked her to read "just to Chapter 2." When they were done he said, "Now keep reading."

Another day, he was asked to leave his *Read with Me!* session to attend a small group guidance session. He said to the counselor, "She has got to finish this page. I'll come in a minute." When they had finished reading the page he said, "I'll come back when I'm done." Later, he returned to the *Read with Me!* room and told the AmeriCorps member, "I want to show you my favorite part."

May 9

One day he came to his *Read with Me!* session early and knocked on the window to come in. He has developed a new interest in wordless books and writes his own stories for wordless books at home. He now looks carefully at what is happening before and after a picture in these books before telling about the story. He begs for more books all the time and is smiling during the whole *Read with Me!* session.

May 16

His interest in different kinds of books keeps expanding, as does his confidence about reading. He often says, "I want to do it myself." He asked to take a book back to his classroom so he could read it to his class. After reading to the class, he was just beaming and said, "I only got half way through it, can I keep it longer?"

May 23

He expressed a concern that he had been absent and wondered if he could have extra time to make up for it.

May 30

The child came in from recess one day and knocked on the *Read with Me!* room door, asking, "Are you going to come and get me? I'm ready. Are you going to come and get me?" The AmeriCorps member directed him to put away his coat and tell his teacher, then to come back. When he had done this, he returned and said, "OK, I'm ready. I love these books. I'm getting smart. I can read these!"

From Reading Together in Kindergarten Handbook (pp. 59–60) by Helen Davig and Cynthia Jacobson, Instructional Services Department, 1998, Holmen, WI: Holmen School District. © 1998 by the Holmen School District. Adapted with permission.

Parent Permission Letter

Dear Parents,

The School District of _____ offers its *Read with Me!* program to preschool or kindergarten children who could benefit from time with books and related activities.

During this time, your child, _____, will spend 15 minutes daily with an adult *Read with Me!* facilitator. _____ will have an opportunity to select books, participate in various reading activities, and grow in his or her desire to learn to read. Part of this one-to-one program includes parents watching five videotaped lessons of their child, reading the take-home book and other books with their child, and responding to monthly surveys.

Please return this slip to your child's teacher by _____.

The attached brochure may answer any questions. If you have additional questions about your child's participation in this program, please contact me at this phone number: _____.

Sincerely,

Read with Me! Coordinator

I give my permission for my child, _____, to participate in the *Read with Me!* program and to be videotaped as part of that program. I understand that this tape will not be used for commercial purposes, but only for the at-home component of this program.

Signature _____   Phone Number _____

Please return to your child's teacher by _____.

From *Reading Together in Kindergarten Handbook* (p. 20) by Helen Davig and Cynthia Jacobson, Instructional Services Department, 1998, Holmen, WI: Holmen School District. © 1998 by the Holmen School District. Adapted with permission.

Parent Conference Letter

Dear Parent,

Thank you for returning the parent permission letter for the *Read with Me!* program, including take-home books and family videotapes.

We hope that the *Read with Me!* brochure provided you with information and answered any questions you might have had.

We look forward to meeting you at parent conferences on _____ at _____ in Room _____.

Sincerely,

Read with Me! Facilitator

From *Reading Together in Kindergarten Handbook* (p. 25) by Helen Davig and Cynthia Jacobson, Instructional Services Department, 1998, Holmen, WI: Holmen School District. © 1998 by the Holmen School District. Adapted with permission.

Read with Me!

Read with Me! Strategies

Echo Reading

Paired Reading

Questioning

Predicting

Wordless Books

Reader's Theatre

What Parents Have Said about Read with Me!

"This is a great program."

"My child enjoys the books."

"I think the video was a great idea."

"The whole family enjoyed watching the video and reading the books."

"My child really wants to learn how to read."

"Books are a favorite free-time activity."

"This is a good idea. I like it."

"My child really enjoyed this program."

"My child talks about it all the time!"

From *Reading Together in Kindergarten Handbook* (pp. 21–22) by Helen Davig and Cynthia Jacobson, Instructional Services Department, 1998, Holmen, WI: Holmen School District. © 1998 by the Holmen School District. Adapted with permission.

Read with Me! Is:

- Daily
- Individual
- 15 minutes
- Child centered
- Books at school
- Take-home books
- Videos
- Family centered
- Home activities

What Happens at School?

A brochure about the program and a permission form are sent home.

Each child who returns the permission form is assigned a *Read with Me!* facilitator.

Every day the child chooses two to three books he or she would like to read with the facilitator.

Facilitator and child videotape a lesson that will be sent home with a take-home book five times a year.

Each child gets to keep the book sent home with the videotape. This is at no cost to your family.

What Happens at Home?

Parents give permission for their child to participate in the program and for their child to be videotaped five times.

Parent and child watch all five segments of the videotape together at least once.

Parents follows reading suggestions in the front cover of the take-home book when reading with their child.

Parents practice the strategies taught on the videos with other books.

Child keeps the books sent home.

Parents fill out a video evaluation survey after each new segment.

Parents return the video and survey to child's teacher.

From *Reading Together in Kindergarten Handbook* (pp. 21–22) by Helen Davig and Cynthia Jacobson, Instructional Services Department, 1998, Holmen, WI: Holmen School District. © 1998 by the Holmen School District. Adapted with permission.

Read with Me! © 2002 Thinking Publications
Duplication permitted for educational use only.

Student Interest Survey

_____ _____
Student   Teacher

_____ _____
Facilitator   Date

Circle One: PRE   POST

Interview the student and record the responses below.

1. Do you like listening to stories?

2. What is your favorite book?

3. What can you tell me about books?

4. What are some books you have at home?

5. Who reads books to you at home?

6. Can you read?

7. Why do people read?

From *Reading Together in Kindergarten Handbook* (p. 24) by Helen Davig and Cynthia Jacobson, Instructional Services Department, 1998, Holmen, WI: Holmen School District. © 1998 by the Holmen School District. Adapted with permission.

Daily Facilitator Log

Student: _____

Facilitator: _____

Teacher: _____

Response Key
1 = Loved It
2 = Liked It
3 = OK
4 = Inattentive
5 = Didn't Like It

Date	Book	Response	Comments

From *Reading Together in Kindergarten Handbook* (p. 23) by Helen Davig and Cynthia Jacobson, Instructional Services Department, 1998, Holmen, WI: Holmen School District. © 1998 by the Holmen School District. Adapted with permission.

Take-Home Book List

NOTE: Detailed reference information and purchasing information for each of the books listed below can be found in Appendix B and Appendix C, respectively.

Assessment Book:
Ice Cream

Take-Home Books:

Echo Reading
I Went Walking
Sue Williams

Paired Reading
The Secret Birthday Message
Eric Carle

Questioning/Predicting
Is Your Mama a Llama?
Deborah Guarino

Wordless Books
Deep in the Forest
Brinton Turkle

Reader's Theatre
The Doorbell Rang
Pat Hutchins

Chapter Books
Dinosaurs Before Dark
Mary Pope Osborne

Alternate Books:

Echo Reading
Down by the Bay
Raffi

Paired Reading
Mortimer
Robert Munsch

Questioning/Predicting
There's a Nightmare in My Closet
Mercer Mayer

Wordless Books
Frog, Where Are You?
Mercer Mayer

Reader's Theatre
City Storm
Rebel Williams

Chapter Books
Additional titles from the *Magic Treehouse Series*
Mary Pope Osborne

From *Reading Together in Kindergarten Handbook* (p. 8) by Helen Davig and Cynthia Jacobson, Instructional Services Department, 1998, Holmen, WI: Holmen School District. © 1998 by the Holmen School District. Adapted with permission.

Parent Video Evaluation
Echo Reading

Dear *Read with Me!* Parents,

Thanks for your participation in the *Read with Me!* program. We are very pleased to have so many parents taking part in this home-school project.

Inside this bag you will find the videotape with your child's *Read with Me!* activity and your copy of *I Went Walking* with reading suggestions on the label. We hope that you enjoy viewing the videotape and completing the reading activities with your child. After you finish the activity with your child, please answer the following questions and return this sheet with the video. Please do **not** rewind the video.

If you have questions, please contact me at _____.

Sincerely,

Read with Me! Facilitator

1. Did you watch the videotape with your child?   Yes   No

2. Which suggested reading activities did you do while reading the book sent home with your child?
    ___ Read slowly
    ___ Let your child hold the book
    ___ Echo read this book with your child
    ___ Continued echo chanting using the phrase from the book while taking a walk

3. Which suggested reading activities did you do while reading other books with your child?
    ___ Read slowly
    ___ Let your child hold the book
    ___ Echo read this book with your child
    ___ Continued echo chanting each phrase throughout the book
    ___ Tried echo singing the book

4. Additional comments or questions: _____
    _____

Your name (optional): _____

Please return this form and your videotape to your child's teacher by _____.

From *Reading Together in Kindergarten Handbook* (p. 45) by Helen Davig and Cynthia Jacobson, Instructional Services Department, 1998, Holmen, WI: Holmen School District. © 1998 by the Holmen School District. Adapted with permission.

Parent Video Evaluation
Paired Reading

Dear *Read with Me!* Parents,

Thank you for responding to the questions that came home with the last videotape. Inside your child's bag you will find the videotape with your child's *Read with Me!* activity and your copy of *The Secret Birthday Message* with reading suggestions on the label. We hope you enjoy the videotape and completing the paired reading activity with your child.

After you finish the activity with your child, please answer the following questions and return this sheet with the video. Please do **not** rewind the video.

If you have questions, please contact me at _____.

Sincerely,

Read with Me! Facilitator

1. Did you watch the videotape with your child?   Yes   No

2. Which suggested reading activities did you do while reading the book sent home with your child?
   ___ Read the secret message note and let your child guess what each shape might be
   ___ Encouraged your child to look at the picture clues and say each shape word
   ___ Moved your finger under each sentence as you read
   ___ Helped your child write his or her own "secret message" by using picture clues

3. Which suggested reading activities did you do while reading other books with your child?
   ___ Encouraged your child to read along with you
   ___ Moved your finger under repeated phrases in the story
   ___ Paused before repeated phrases to let your child say them with you
   ___ Asked your child to sing the "clang, clang" chant with you (if you read *Mortimer*)

4. Additional comments or questions: _____
   _____

Your name (optional): _____

Please return this form and your videotape to your child's teacher by _____.

From *Reading Together in Kindergarten Handbook* (p. 46) by Helen Davig and Cynthia Jacobson, Instructional Services Department, 1998, Holmen, WI: Holmen School District. © 1998 by the Holmen School District. Adapted with permission.

Parent Video Evaluation
Questioning and Predicting

Dear *Read with Me!* Parents,

Thank you for responding to the questions that came home with the last videotape. Inside your child's bag you will find the videotape with your child's *Read with Me!* activity and your copy of *Is Your Mama a Llama?* with reading suggestions on the label. We hope you enjoy the videotape and completing the questioning and predicting activity with your child.

After you finish the activity with your child, please answer the following questions and return this sheet with the video. Please do **not** rewind the video.

If you have questions, please contact me at _____.

Sincerely,

Read with Me! Facilitator

---

1. Did you watch the videotape with your child?   Yes   No

2. Which suggested reading activities did you do while reading the book sent home with your child?
   ___ Stopped reading to ask your child what might happen next
   ___ Praised your child for all his or her predictions

3. Which suggested reading activities did you do while reading other books with your child?
   ___ Stopped reading to ask your child what might happen next
   ___ Praised your child for all his or her predictions

4. Additional comments or questions: _____
   _____

Your name (optional): _____

Please return this form and your videotape to your child's teacher by _____.

From *Reading Together in Kindergarten Handbook* (p. 47) by Helen Davig and Cynthia Jacobson, Instructional Services Department, 1998, Holmen, WI: Holmen School District. © 1998 by the Holmen School District. Adapted with permission.

Parent Video Evaluation
Wordless Books

Dear *Read with Me!* Parents,

Thank you for responding to the questions that came home with the last videotape. Inside your child's bag you will find the videotape with your child's *Read with Me!* activity and your copy of *Deep in the Forest* with reading suggestions on the label. We hope you enjoy the videotape and completing the wordless book activity with your child.

After you finish the activity with your child, please answer the following questions and return this sheet with the video. Please do **not** rewind the video.

If you have questions, please contact me at _____.

Sincerely,

Read with Me! Facilitator

1. Did you watch the videotape with your child?   Yes   No

2. Which suggested reading activities did you do while reading the book sent home with your child?
   ___ Read through the book and talked about the actions of the story
   ___ Reread the book and asked your child to tell you about one event on each page
   ___ Used Post-it notes to write your child's exact words for each page
   ___ Reread your child's words and watched him or her discover that what is said can be written and read again

3. Which suggested reading activities did you do while reading other books with your child?
   ___ Read through the book and talked about the actions of the story
   ___ Reread the book and asked your child to tell you about one event on each page
   ___ Used Post-it notes to write your child's exact words for each page
   ___ Reread your child's words and watched him or her discover that what is said can be written and read again

4. Additional comments or questions: _____

   _____

Your name (optional): _____

Please return this form and your videotape to your child's teacher by _____.

From *Reading Together in Kindergarten Handbook* (p. 48) by Helen Davig and Cynthia Jacobson, Instructional Services Department, 1998, Holmen, WI: Holmen School District. © 1998 by the Holmen School District. Adapted with permission.

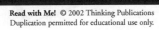

Parent Video Evaluation
Reader's Theatre

Dear *Read with Me!* Parents,

Thank you for responding to the questions that came home with the last videotape. Inside your child's bag you will find the videotape with your child's *Read with Me!* activity and your copy of *The Doorbell Rang* with reading suggestions on the label. We hope you enjoy the videotape and completing the reader's theatre activity with your child.

After you finish the activity with your child, please answer the following questions and return this sheet with the video. Please do **not** rewind the video.

If you have questions, please contact me at _____.

Sincerely,

Read with Me! Facilitator

---

1. Did you watch the videotape with your child?   Yes   No

2. Which suggested reading activities did you do while reading the book sent home with your child?
   ___ Read the story several times
   ___ Asked your child to join in with you by saying the repeated phrases
   ___ Gathered simple props for acting out the story
   ___ Had fun acting out the story together

3. Which suggested reading activities did you do while reading other books with your child?
   ___ Read the story several times
   ___ Helped your child gather simple props or make stick puppets for acting out the story
   ___ Used your child's natural interests in play to act out the story
   ___ Had fun acting out the story together

4. Additional comments or questions: _____
   _____

Your name (optional): _____

Please return this form and your videotape to your child's teacher by _____.

From *Reading Together in Kindergarten Handbook* (p. 49) by Helen Davig and Cynthia Jacobson, Instructional Services Department, 1998, Holmen, WI: Holmen School District. © 1998 by the Holmen School District. Adapted with permission.

Read with Me!
Success Report

Student: _____

Date: _____

Favorite Books:

Reading Participation:

Other Comments:

From *Reading Together in Kindergarten Handbook* (p. 27) by Helen Davig and Cynthia Jacobson, Instructional Services Department, 1998, Holmen, WI: Holmen School District. © 1998 by the Holmen School District. Adapted with permission.

Read with Me!
Success Report

(Sample)

Student: Tabatha

Date: _____

Favorite Books:
- *The Very Busy Spider*
- *Brown Bear, Brown Bear*
- *The Very Hungry Caterpillar*
- *Jump, Frog, Jump*

Reading Participation:
- Excellent listener
- Does great with reading participation
- Reads story patterns on her own from memory
- Always joins in and reads with me from memory

Other Comments:

Tabatha's confidence has really grown over the past month. She is always very enthusiastic about reading books and is an excellent listener. She is very determined to do a good job and tries very hard to do her best. She will read books to me that she is familiar with from memory, such as *Brown Bear, Brown Bear*. She does great! I enjoy reading with Tabatha; she is a lot of fun.

From *Reading Together in Kindergarten Handbook* (p. 28) by Helen Davig and Cynthia Jacobson, Instructional Services Department, 1998, Holmen, WI: Holmen School District. © 1998 by the Holmen School District. Adapted with permission.

Read with Me! Success Award

CONGRATULATIONS

_____

You have done an excellent job this year!

You Have Read ____ Books!

KEEP ON READING!

From *Reading Together in Kindergarten Handbook* (p. 35) by Helen Davig and Cynthia Jacobson, Instructional Services Department, 1998, Holmen, WI: Holmen School District. © 1998 by the Holmen School District. Adapted with permission.

Student Achievement Checklist

Student _____ Teacher _____

Facilitator _____ Date _____

Circle One: PRE   POST

Indicate the skills the student demonstrates as secure (consistently and repeatedly observed) or nonsecure (inconsistently observed).

Emergent/Transitional Readers	Secure	Nonsecure
Understands concepts of print (how to hold a book, left to right flow)	_____	_____
Demonstrates an awareness of words and letters	_____	_____
Demonstrates beginning development of letter-sound relationships	_____	_____
Demonstrates beginning awareness of story structure	_____	_____
Demonstrates beginning awareness of stability of print	_____	_____
Matches voice/print correlations	_____	_____
Uses pictures to develop some sight word and letter recognition	_____	_____
Begins to develop decoding strategies (initial letters, picture cues, chunking)	_____	_____
Retells stories with some detail	_____	_____
Knows letters and their corresponding sounds	_____	_____

From *Reading Together in Kindergarten Handbook* (p. 32) by Helen Davig and Cynthia Jacobson, Instructional Services Department, 1998, Holmen, WI: Holmen School District. © 1998 by the Holmen School District. Adapted with permission.

Section IV

Speech-Language Intervention

Read with Me!

CONTENTS

Overview 113
Goals 114
Meeting Specific Goals and Objectives. 114

Section IV

OVERVIEW

Incorporating *Read with Me!* strategies and books into speech-language intervention is clearly an exemplar of best practice in the field, from both a theoretical and a practical viewpoint. The notion of a reciprocal relationship between the child and the environment is central to social theories of language learning (e.g., Bruner, 1983; Vygotsky, 1978). From this perspective, children operate as participants in various interactive contexts throughout the time that they are learning language. Language, therefore, does not develop in isolation, but is heavily dependent on the social context in which it is learned and used. Bricker (1986) expanded on this view by arguing that children's participation in real conversations and real interactions allows them to gain experience with language that cannot be duplicated in a structured lesson targeting a particular discrete language skill.

Obviously, reading with children is an excellent example of a "real" interaction. In fact, book reading has been described as the ideal context for developing communication skills because its is much more representative of the natural interactions between parent and child (Crowe et al., 2000). Consequently, the strategies and books associated with the *Read with Me!* program clearly have the potential to be much more effective in promoting increases in communication than more typical clinician-directed intervention sessions that tend to be stripped of the natural context.

On the other hand, the clinician is still able to structure the intervention in order to target specific communication goals and objectives as developed by the IEP team. Thus, on the continuum of naturalness as defined by Fey (1986), intervention using *Read with Me!* strategies represents a hybrid approach that allows both the clinician and the child to have some level of control over the activity.

The practical applications of using *Read with Me!* in speech-language intervention are both numerous and exciting. Clearly, newly learned skills are more easily generalized to environments outside of the intervention room because of the strong contextual support provided by reading interactions. The clinician can capitalize on this by developing activities to support communication and language using *Read with Me!* strategies and recommended books.

For instance, books that a child is reading in the classroom can be preread with the speech-language pathologist using echo or paired reading. This provides several important benefits. First, becoming familiar with the book prior to having to read it in the classroom setting increases the probability of better performance in that setting (that is, the child can read the book better.) This increased performance level can bolster the child's self-confidence and reduce the stress related to reading. In addition, because the child knows the book, he or she can pay more attention to the learning opportunities that are going on in the classroom than on working so hard just to try to get through the actual reading. This is a means of stretching cognitive resources that allows the child to participate more fully in the learning experience (Shatz, 1983).

Another positive aspect of *Read with Me!* is that the cost of materials is minimal. Generally, softcover versions of the suggested books are less than $5 each, with Big Books averaging around $25 each. Many of the books listed on the *Read with Me!* booklists (see Appendix B) can be found on the shelves of the school library (and Big Books can often be borrowed from a Kindergarten teacher). With the bare bones budgets that many professionals are working with, this is a definite plus.

GOALS

- Provide children who have communication disorders with meaningful reading experiences that promote increased proficiency in both the oral and written language domains.
- Meet the goals and objectives established in a child's IEP through the application of *Read with Me!* strategies and recommended books.
- Provide speech-language pathologists with theoretically sound and clinically appropriate strategies for remediating communication.

MEETING SPECIFIC GOALS AND OBJECTIVES

Read with Me! strategies and books can be used to address a variety of goals and objectives related to communication. Obviously, the options for applying the *Read with Me!* program books and strategies are as varied and unique as the children on caseloads. In this section, the potential for using various components of *Read with Me!* to meet goals and objectives established for children with communication disorders is demonstrated. These ideas show the robust potential of using the *Read with Me!* strategies in clinical applications, and they will also activate the creative gene that lurks in the souls of all speech-language pathologists! Note that books that support each of the strategies listed (e.g., echo reading, paired reading, and reader's theatre) as well as references for each of the individual books listed in this section can be found in Appendix B.

Verbalization

- Simple books with exciting pictures and simple text are best for encouraging children to join in the reading interaction, such as:

    Dinosaur Roar!
    In the Small, Small Pond
    Parade

- Reader's theatre techniques can help a child become actively engaged in the reading interaction. This can help stimulate oral participation.

    There Was an Old Lady Who Swallowed a Fly
    We're Going on a Bear Hunt
    Clap Your Hands
    From Head to Toe
    Hand Rhymes

Utterance Length and Complexity

- Echo reading provides a verbal model and a chance for a child to repeat the model within a natural context. Clinicians can select books targeting specific syntactic or semantic constructs related to the needs of the child.

- Paired reading provides children with opportunities to use longer and more complex sentence construction than they might be able to produce spontaneously. Again, the clinician can tailor the type of paired reading to the needs of each individual child. That is, they might read by the word, by the phrase, or even by the page.

- Open-ended questions encourage a child to use longer, more complex utterances. Generally, a fact-based question (e.g., "Who is under the bed?") requires only a short one- or two- word response, while an open-ended question (e.g., "Why do you think the monster is hiding under the bed?") encourages a longer response. In the same way, encouraging the child to predict what might happen next in a story often stimulates a longer, more complex verbalization.

    The Pig Who Ran a Red Light
    The Doorbell Rang
    Sheep in a Jeep

- The open-ended format of a wordless book reading interaction allows children to make up their own verbal text. Expansions and recasts can be used to encourage longer and more complex language with minimal intrusion on the natural reading interaction.

Tuesday
Creepy Castle
The Grey Lady and the Strawberry Snatcher

Vocabulary Development

- For preschoolers, books that provide rich vocabulary paired with pictures and other cues should be chosen. Books that are especially good include:

  Opposites!
  Dinosaur Roar!
  Bears in Pairs
  In the Small, Small Pond

- For older children with constrained vocabularies, books with a highly interesting story line, lots of humor, or that target a child's special interest areas should be used. This often encourages them to think about the words they do not know, use the picture and context cues, or even ask the clinician for clarification. Consider using:

  Where the Sidewalk Ends
  The Stinky Cheeseman and Other Fairly Stupid Tales
  Eye Witness: Sharks
  Dogs Don't Wear Sneakers
  101 Easy-to-Do Magic Tricks
  Who Took My Hairy Toe?
  Lunch

Metalinguistic Skills

- Phonological awareness can be developed with books that have strong rhythm, rhyme, and repetition, such as those used for echo and paired reading. The following are especially appropriate:

  I Heard, Said the Bird
  Jamberry
  Hop on Pop
  Pig in a Wig
  Sheep in a Jeep
  Tumble, Bumble
  "What Is That?" Said the Cat?

Section IV

- An understanding of syllabification can be facilitated by taking turns pointing to the syllables rather than to the words when reading aloud together.

- Counting the words in a sentence can help children learn that sentences are made up of words.

- Books that help develop figurative language skills should be used, such as:

    Quick as a Cricket
    The King Who Rained
    Chocolate Moose for Dinner
    Velcome

Critical Thinking Skills

- Answering open-ended questions and predicting are very effective in promoting critical thinking skills. Great books to use for this include:

    It Looked Like Spilt Milk
    June 29, 1999
    The Little Mouse, the Red Ripe Strawberry, and the Big Hungry Bear
    Two Bad Ants
    Miss Nelson Is Missing
    Look-Alikes

- Books that have improbable themes can encourage children to talk about why the themes are silly or impossible. Consider using:

    Animals Should Definitely Not Wear Clothing
    Bark, George!
    The Cow Who Wouldn't Come Down
    Dogs Don't Wear Sneakers
    Good Dog, Carl
    The Mitten
    The Pig Who Ran a Red Light
    Silly Sally
    The Silly, Slimy, Smelly, Hairy Book
    Tuesday
    Will's Mammoth

- Books that are written from an unexpected viewpoint should be considered, such as:

    Deep in the Forest

Read with Me!

Each Peach, Pear, Plum
The Jolly Postman
Prince Cinders
The Three Pigs
The Three Wolves and the Big Bad Pig

- Books that have very few words encourage children to "fill in the blanks" and to understand what the author is trying to communicate. You might try:

In the Small, Small Pond
One Afternoon
Rosie's Walk
Sheep on a Ship
Yo! Yes?

Pragmatic Skills

- Echo reading and paired reading promote turn-taking skills.

- Reading interactions that incorporate *Read with Me!* strategies encourage joint attending.

- Reader's theatre books that encourage body movement support the development of paired action.

- *Read with Me!* strategies and recommended books encourage increased attending, both in terms of length of time attending and the level of attending. The following books are especially helpful:

Dinosaur Stomp
One Duck Stuck
Silly Sally
The Silly, Slimy, Smelly, Hairy Book

- Books that are built on or around a specific social premise or problem should be considered, for example.

Marsupial Sue
A Porcupine Named Fluffy
The Okay Book
Yo! Yes?

Section IV

Articulation and Phonology

- Newly learned sounds can be practiced within the natural context of shared book reading using any of the *Read with Me!* strategies.

- Books that provide minimal contrast practice should be used, such as:

  Jamberry
  Pig in a Wig
  Miss Bindergarten Gets Ready for Kindergarten
  Mrs. McNosh Hangs Up Her Wash
  Sheep in a Jeep
  Fox in Socks
  Hop on Pop

- Some books are especially good for children with speech-sound errors because they help them understand that other people have difficulties too.

  Hurray for Wodney Wat
  Leo the Late Bloomer
  Grandpa's Teeth

- Echo reading provides a good model of the targeted sounds. The clinician can stress the targeted sound within the text before the child echoes it (CLINICIAN: I **w**ent **w**alking; CHILD: I went walking).

Fluent Speech

- The rhythmic cadence and repetitive phrases of books that are used for paired reading (see Appendix B) are excellent for promoting fluent speech.

- A non-judgmental atmosphere reduces stress to facilitate fluency.

- Engaging the child's whole body as well as the oral mechanism during reader's theatre activities may encourage the child to be more fluent.

Good Vocal Hygiene

- The relaxed atmosphere of *Read with Me!* book reading interactions can assist a child in relaxation of the oral and vocal structures. Choose books that project a more relaxed mood, such as:

  Goodnight, Moon
  Time for Bed

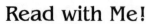

Read with Me!

- Echo reading can be modified to include repetition of a targeted skill, such as using a yawn-sigh (i.e., a technique that encourages easy onset; the child yawns and then exhales gently with a light phonation), as well as the printed words (clinician models yawn-sign and then says "Dinosaur roar"; the child produces yawn-sign and then echoes the words).

- Using targeted vocal hygiene skills, such as talking at an appropriate loudness level, can be practiced during joint reading (i.e., the child reads at the same loudness level as the professional).

Appendices

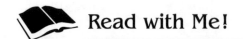 Read with Me!

CONTENTS

Appendix A: Parent Literacy Training Study 123
Appendix B: Expanded Book Lists. 126
Appendix C: Purchasing Information 161
Appendix D: Overhead Presentation. 162
Appendix E: Frequently Asked Questions 170

PARENT LITERACY TRAINING STUDY

Introduction

This study investigated the effects of parent literacy training on the expressive language and literacy development of preschool children. In addition, changes in parents' reading behaviors and attitudes about reading with their children after receiving literacy training were examined.

Although schools can do much to build literacy skills, numerous investigations have suggested that exposing children to developmentally appropriate activities related to reading and writing during the preschool years has a substantial impact on getting children off to a better start once formal reading instruction begins (Cole, 1995; Fey, Catts, and Larrivee, 1995).

Methods

Participants

Twenty-four preschool-aged children and their parents were randomly assigned to either an experimental (n=12) or delayed treatment control (n=12) group. Children with and without identified language delays took part in the investigation; however, children with frank neurological, cognitive, or emotional delays were excluded.

Participant Characteristics

Variable	Experimental (n=12) M	SD	Control (n=12) M	SD
Age (in months)	46.25	6.78	44.25	6.44
MLU	3.95	.67	3.86	.63
SES (Maternal years in school)	15.00	2.48	15.58	3.44

Treatment

Three 60-minute training workshops, one each week for three consecutive weeks, were provided to parents of children in the experimental group. Two strategies were introduced each week through direct instruction, practice with specific books, and discussion of the rationale for each strategy. Parents were further provided with written information, books, and materials to support the use of the strategies in the home setting.

Strategies Trained

Echo Reading	Parent reads text Child repeats text
Paired Reading	Parent reads a portion of text Child completes the text
Questioning	Parent uses open-ended questions to encourage verbalization
Predicting	Parent uses prediction cues to encourage verbalization and critical thinking
Wordless Books	Parent and child engage in literacy activities using books without words
Reader's Theatre	Parent and child engage in dramatization activities that reinforce the story

Read with Me!

Experimental Variables

To examine performance of each of the targeted variables, videotapes of parent-child reading interactions (two books at each interval) at pretest and three weeks following the final training session (a total of six weeks later) were collected. Differences between groups on three child variables, Number of Different Words (NDW), Number of Verbal Participations, and Percentage Attending Behavior. One parent behavior variable, Percentage of Open-Ended Questions, and one combined variable, Ratio of Parent to Child Utterances, were compared.

Results

Results of this investigation suggest that children whose parents received training demonstrated statistically significant increases across all targeted variables. In addition, parental behaviors were also modified.

Number of Different Words
Used by Children during Parent-Child Reading Interaction

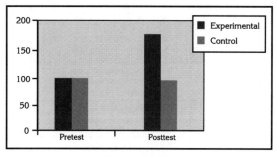

Number of Verbal Participations
Demonstrated by Children during Parent-Child Reading Interactions

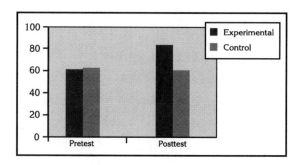

Percentage Attending Behavior
Demonstrated by Children during Parent-Child Reading Interactions

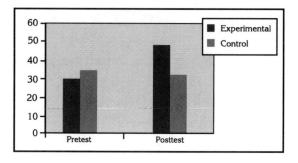

Percentage of Open-Ended Questions
Used by Parent during Parent-Child Reading Interactions

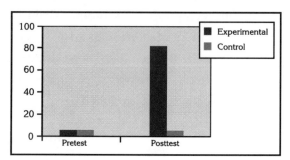

Appendix A

Ratio of Parent to Child Utterances
during Parent-Child Reading Interactions

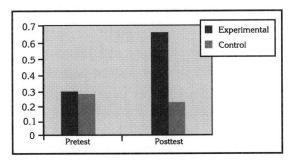

Parent Perceptions of Children's Reading Skills

Parents were asked to rate specific behaviors related to their perceptions of their child's behaviors related to reading at pretest and again at posttest. Results suggest parents of children in the experimental groups demonstrated a marked overall positive increase in their attitudes and perceptions about reading with their children.

Discussion

These outcomes supplement previous findings suggesting that parent training can evoke changes in both parent and child behaviors. In addition, the hypothesis that parents who are instructed to use certain language and literacy stimulation techniques will demonstrate positive changes in their attitudes and perceptions about reading with their children was upheld.

These results support the practice of using parent mediated intervention strategies to facilitate increases in language and early literacy skills.

From *The Effects of Parental Training on the Language and Literacy Behaviors of Children,* by S. Robertson, D. Smith, and M. Sollenberger, November, 2001, Poster session presented at the national convention of the American Speech-Language-Hearing Association, New Orleans, LA. © 2001 by S. Robertson, D. Smith, and M. Sollenberger. Adapted with permission.

Appendix B

EXPANDED BOOK LISTS

The books included in these lists are favorites of the authors and the families and educators who have participated in various workshops related to the *Read with Me!* program. The books are divided into categories that coincide with the *Read with Me!* strategies and genres. Most of them are further divided by age (wordless books and reader's theatre can be adapted for any age). Note that children of all ages can enjoy the simpler books, but books for children ages 4 and older would not be appropriate for babies and toddlers.

Lists of books that foster more academically based skills (such as phonics and math) and those that target older readers (age 8 and above) are also provided. However, do not be afraid to try any of the books with any child. Children quickly develop favorites they will want to revisit over and over again. On the other hand, do not force a book on a child who does not seem to enjoy it. Remember to always keep reading fun and stress free!

Echo Reading

Across the Stream
Mirra Ginsburg, 1991, New York: Mulberry Books

Bears in Pairs
Niki Yekai, 1987, New York: Simon and Schuster

A Bug, a Bear, and a Boy Series
David McPhail, New York: Scholastic

A Bug, a Bear, and a Boy (1998)

A Bug, a Bear, and a Boy at Home (1997)

A Bug, a Bear, and a Boy Go to School (1999)

A Bug, a Bear, and a Boy Paint a Picture (1998)

A Bug, a Bear, and a Boy, Plant a Garden (1997)

A Bug, a Bear, and a Boy, Play Hide-and-Seek (1997)

Clifford's Word Book
Norman Bridwell, 1990, New York: Scholastic

Dinner Time!
Jan Pienkowski, 2000, Issaquah, WA: Piggy Toes Press

Dinosaur Roar!
Paul Strickland and Henrieta Strickland, 1994, New York: Penguin Books

Down by the Bay
Raffi, 1999, New York: Crown Books

Flying
Donald Crews, 1989, New York: Mulberry Books

How Do You Say It Today, Jessie Bear?
Nancy Carlstrom, 1992, New York: Simon and Schuster

In the Small, Small Pond
Denise Fleming, 1993, New York: Henry Holt

In the Tall, Tall Grass
Denise Fleming, 1995, New York: Henry Holt

I Went Walking
Sue Williams, 1992, Orlando, FL: Harcourt Brace

Jesse Bear, What Will You Wear?
Nancy Carlstrom, 1996, New York: Simon and Schuster

Let's Go Visiting
Sue Williams, 1998, Orlando, FL: Harcourt Brace

One Afternoon
Yumi Heo, 1998, New York: Foresman

One Fish, Two Fish, Red Fish, Blue Fish
Dr. Suess, 1981, New York: Random House

Opposites
Mary Novik and Sybel Harlin, 2001, Surry Hills, NSW, Australia: Little Hare Books

Parade
Donald Crews, 1986, New York: Mulberry Books

Pizza Party
Grace Maccarone, 1994, New York: Cartwheel Books

Quick as a Cricket
Audrey Wood, 1998, Swindon, England: Child's Play

Rosie's Walk
Pat Hutchins, 1983, New York: Foresman

Slower Than a Snail
Anne Screiber, 1995, New York: Scholastic

Spot's Big Book of Words
Eric Hill, 1995, New York: Puffin Books

Tidy Titch
Pat Hutchins, 1995, New York: Mulberry Books

Truck
Donald Crews, 1997, New York: Mulberry Books

Up and Down on the Merry-Go-Round
John Archanbault, 1991, New York: Holt

Yo! Yes?
Chris Raschka, 1998, New York: Orchard Books

Appendix B

Paired Reading

Babies, Toddlers, Preschoolers, and Everyone

Brown Bear, Brown Bear, What Do You See?
Bill Martin Jr., 1992, New York: Holt

The Carrot Seed
Ruth Frauss, 1993, New York: HarperFestival

Chicken Soup with Rice
Maurice Sendak, 1991, New York: Foresman

Dinosaur Stomp
Paul Strickland and Henrieta Strickland, 1996, New York: Dutton Books

Each Peach, Pear, Plum
Janet Ahlberg, 1986, New York: Foresman

Five Little Monkeys Jumping on the Bed
Eileen Christelow, 1989, Boston: Houghton Mifflin

Here Are My Hands
Bill Martin Jr., 1998, New York: Holt

Jump, Frog, Jump
Robert Kaplan, 1989, New York: Mulberry Books

Love You Until
Lisa McCourt, 1999, New York: Paulist Press.

The Missing Tarts
B.G. Hennessy, 1989, New York: Penguin

Moo, Moo, Brown Cow
Jakki Wood, 1996, New York: Harcourt

Mortimer
Robert Munsch, 1985, New York: Firefly Books

One Duck Stuck
Phyllis Root, 1998, Cambridge, MA: Candlewick Press

Read with Me!

Peanut Butter and Jelly
Nadine Westcott, 1992, New York: Dutton

Peek-a-Boo
Janet Ahlberg, 1997, New York: Viking

Piggies
Audrey Wood, 1991, New York: Harcourt Brace

The Secret Birthday Message
Eric Carle, 1981, Lake in the Hills, IL: Crowell

Silly Sally
Audrey Wood, 1992, New York: Harcourt Brace

Silly Willy
Maryann Cocca-Leffler, 1995, New York: Grosset and Dunlap

Time for Bed
Mem Fox, 1997, New York: Harcourt Brace

Tumble, Bumble
Felicia Bond, 1996, New York: HarperCollins

The Very Busy Spider
Eric Carle, 1994, New York: Scholastic

Where's Baby Tom?
Brian Birchall, 1993, New York: Morrow

Who Said "Moo?"
Mike Artell, 1994, New York: Simon and Schuster

4 Years and Older

Andrew's Loose Tooth
Robert Munsch, 1999, New York: Cartwheel Books

Bunny Trouble
Hans Wilhelm, 2001, New York: Scholastic

Appendix B

The Bus for Us
Suzanne Bloom, 2000, Honesdale, PA: Boyd Mills

Buz
Richard Egielski, 1999, New York: HarperCollins

Caps for Sale
Esphyr Slobodkina, 1987, New York: HarperTrophy

Chicka Chicka Boom Boom
John Archanbault and Bill Martin Jr., 1991, New York: Simon and Schuster

The Cows Are in the Corn
James Young, 1996, New York: Penguin

Dreamsnow
Eric Carle, 2000, New York: Philomel Books

Footprints in the Snow
Cynthia Benjamin, 1994, New York: Cartwheel Books

The Fox Went Out on a Chilly Night
Peter Spier, 1993, New York: Yearling Books

Get Out of Bed
Robert Munsch, 1999, New York: Scholastic

The Happy Hippopatomi
Betsy Everitt, 1992, New York: Harcourt

Here Comes the Snow
Angela Medearis, 1996, New York: Cartwheel Books

A House for Hermit Crab
Eric Carle, 1991, New York: Foresman

It Looked Like Spilt Milk
Charles G. Shaw, 1988, New York: HarperTrophy

Jamberry
Bruce Degen, 1995, New York: HarperFestival

Read with Me!

Kate Skates
Wendy Blaxland, 1995, New York: Putnam

Love You Forever
Robert Munsch, 1998, New York: Firefly

More or Less a Mess
Sheila Keenan, 1997, New York: Cartwheel Books

My Messy Room
Mary Parkard, 1993, New York: Cartwheel Books

My Tooth is About To Fall Out
Grace Maccarone, 1995, New York: Cartwheel Books

One Gorilla
Atsuko Morozumi, 1993, New York: Sunburst

One Snowy Day
Jeffery Scherer, 1997, New York: Cartwheel Books

Pigs Ahoy
David McPhail, 1998, New York: Puffin Books

Pigs a Plenty, Pigs Galore
David McPhail, 1997, New York: Puffin Books

Roosters Off to See the World
Eric Carle, 1999, New York: Aladdin

Show and Tell
Robert Munsch, 1991, Toronto, Canada: Annick Press

The Silly, Slimy, Smelly, Hairy Book
Babette Cole, 2001, London: Random House

Six Creepy Sheep
Judith Engerle, 2001, Honesdale, PA: Boyd Mills

Six Sandy Sheep
Judith Engerle, 1997, Honesdale, PA: Boyd Mills

So Say the Little Monkeys
Nancy Van Laan, 1998, New York: Altheneum Press

Six Snowy Sheep
Judith Engerle, 1994, Honesdale, PA: Boyd Mills

The Very Lonely Firefly
Eric Carle, 1999, New York: Philomel Books

The Very Quiet Cricket
Eric Carle, 1997, New York: Putnam

"What Is That?" Said the Cat
Grace Maccarone, 1998, New York: Cartwheel Books

Who Stole the Cookies?
Judith Moffatt, 1996, New York: Grosset and Dunlap

Read with Me!

Questioning and Predicting
Babies, Toddlers, Preschoolers, and Everyone

Better Not Get Wet, Jesse Bear!
Nancy Carlstrom, 1997, New York: Aladdin Books

Boats
Byron Barton, 1998, New York: HarperCollins

Bugs in Space
David Carter, 1997, New York: Simon and Schuster

Corduroy
Don Freeman, 1985, New York: Viking

Dear Zoo
Rod Campbell, 1999, New York: Simon and Schuster

Dinosaur Garden
Liza Donnelly, 1991, New York: Scholastic

Dinosaurs, Dinosaurs
Byron Barton, 1994, New York: HarperFestival

Everyone Hide from Wibbly Pig
Mick Inkpen, 1997, New York: Viking

Fire Engines
Anne Rockwell, 1993, New York: Puffin Books

Harbor
Donald Crews, 1987, New York: Mulberry Books

I Went Walking
Sue Williams, 1992, New York: Harcourt

Inside Freight Train
Donald Crews, 2001, New York: Mulberry Books

Is Your Mama a Llama?
Deborah Guarino, 1989, New York: Scholastic

Lift a Rock, Find a Bug
Chris Santoro, 1993, New York: Random House

The Little Mouse, the Red Ripe Strawberry, and the Big Hungry Bear
Don Wood, 1998, Swindon, England: Child's Play

The Look Book
Tana Hoban, 1997, New York: Greenwillow

Look! Look! Look!
Tana Hoban, 1998, New York: Scholastic

Lunch
Denise Fleming, 1998, New York: Holt

Mary Wore Her Red Dress
Merle Peek, 1995, Boston: Houghton Mifflin

Messy Moose
Lois Bick, 1998, New York: Sandlier

Never Babysit the Hippopotamuses
Doug Johnson, 1997, New York: Owlet

The Okay Book
Todd Parr, 1999, New York: Little, Brown

Open the Barn Door
Chris Santoro, 1993, New York: Random House

Rosie's Walk
Pat Hutchins, 1998, New York: Little Simon

Says Who?
David A. Carter, 1993, New York: Simon and Schuster

Sheep in a Jeep
Nancy Shaw, 1997, Boston: Houghton Mifflin

Sheep in a Shop
Nancy Shaw, 1997, Boston: Houghton Mifflin

Sheep on a Ship
Nancy Shaw, 1992, Boston: Houghton Mifflin

Sheep Out to Eat!
Nancy Shaw, 1995, Boston: Houghton Mifflin

Sheep Trick or Treat
Nancy Shaw, 2000, Boston: Houghton Mifflin

The Smallest Stegosaurus
Lynn Sweat, 1995, New York: Puffin

The Snowy Day
Ezra Jack Keats, 1996, New York: Viking

Spot Series
Eric Hill, New York: Putnam

Spot Goes to the Beach (1995)

Spot Goes to the Park (1991)

Spot Goes to School (2001)

Spot Sleeps Over (1996)

Where's Spot (2000)

Trains
Anne Rockwell, 1993, New York: Penguin

Waiting for the Bus
Barry Small, 2001, London: Tango Books

What Game Shall We Play?
Pat Hutchins, 1995, New York: Mulberry Books

Where Is Maisy?
Lucy Cousins, 1999, Cambridge, MA: Candlewick Press

Where the Wild Things Are
Maurice Sendak, 1988, New York: HarperTrophy

Where's the Baby?
Pat Hutchins, 1999, New York: Mulberry Books

Ages 4 and Older

Alexander and the Terrible, Horrible, No Good, Very Bad Day
Judith Viorst, 1972, New York: Simon and Schuster

Animals Should Definitely Not Wear Clothing
Judi Barrett, 1970, New York: Aladdin Books

Arthur Series
Marc Brown, New York: Little, Brown

Arthur Baby Sits (1992)
Arthur Goes to Camp (1984)
Arthur Writes a Story (1999)
Arthur's Chicken Pox (1994)
Arthur's Family Vacation (1995)
Arthur's Tooth (1993)

The Bag I'm Taking to Grandma's
Shirley Neitzel, 1998, New York: Mulberry Books

Bark, George!
Jules Feiffer, 1999, New York: HarperCollins

Bubble, Bubble
Mercer Mayer, 1992, New York: Rainbird Press

The Bus for Us
Suzanne Bloom, 2001, Honesdale, PA: Boyd Mills

Buzz, Said the Bee
Wendy Lewison, 1992, New York: Scholastic

Can I Have a Stegosaurus, Mom? Can I? Please?
Lois Grambling, 1998, New York: Troll

City Storm
Rebel Williams, Bothell, WA: Wright Group

Read with Me!

Clifford the Big Red Dog Series
Norman Bridwell, New York: Scholastic

Clifford at the Circus (1989)
Clifford Goes to Hollywood (1990)
Clifford and the Grouchy Neighbors (1989)
Clifford the Small Red Puppy (1990)
Clifford's Birthday Party (1990)
Clifford's Christmas (1987)
Clifford's Family (1984)
Clifford's Thanksgiving Visit (1999)

The Cow Who Wouldn't Come Down
Paul Brett Johnson, 1997, New York: Orchard Books

Dogs Don't Wear Sneakers
Laura Numeroff, 1993, New York: Aladdin

The Doorbell Rang
Pat Hutchins, 1989, Columbus, OH: Pearson Learning

Dos and Don'ts
Todd Parr, 1999, New York: Little, Brown

The Dress I'll Wear to the Party
Shirley Neitzel, 1995, New York: Mulberry Books

The Eyes of Gray Wolf
Jonathan London, 1993, San Francisco: Chronicle Books

Green Eggs and Ham
Dr. Suess, 1960, New York: Random House

I Love You, Stinky Face
Lisa McCourt, 1997, New York: Bridgewater Books

Ice Cream
Wendy Blaxland, 1993, Bothell, WA: Wright Group

If You Give a Moose a Muffin
Felicia Bond and Laura Numeroff, 1991, New York: HarperCollins

If You Give a Mouse a Cookie
Felicia Bond and Laura Numeroff, 1985, New York: HarperCollins

If You Give a Pig a Pancake
Felicia Bond and Laura Numeroff, 1988, New York: HarperCollins

If You Take a Mouse to the Movies
Felicia Bond and Laura Numeroff, 2000, New York: HarperCollins

June 29, 1999
David Wiesner, 1992, New York: Clarion Books

Look-Alikes, Jr.
Joan Steiner, 1999, New York: Little, Brown

The Mitten
Jan Brett, 1996, Boston: Houghton Mifflin

Mr. Cookie Baker
Monica Wellington, 1997, New York: Puffin Books

The Pig Who Ran a Red Light
Paul Brett Johnson, 1999, New York: Orchard Books

The Polar Express
Chris Van Ahlsberg, 1995, Boston: Houghton Mifflin

Shortcut
Donald Crews, 1996, New York: Mulberry Books

Six Creepy Sheep
Judith Engerle, 2001, Honesdale, PA: Boyd Mills

Six Sandy Sheep
Judith Engerle, 1997, Honesdale, PA: Boyd Mills

Six Snowy Sheep
Judith Engerle, 1994, Honesdale, PA: Boyd Mills

The Story of Ferdinand
Munroe Leaf, 1997, New York: Viking

Read with Me!

Thanksgiving Day
Gail Gibbons, 1985, New York: Holiday House

There's a Nightmare in My Closet
Mercer Mayer, 1984, New York: Dial Books

Today I Feel Silly and Other Moods That Make My Day
Jamie Lee Curtis, 1998, New York: HarperCollins

What Do You Do, Dear?
Sesyle Joslin, 1986, New York: HarperTrophy

What Do You Say, Dear?
Sesyle Joslin, 1986, New York: HarperTrophy

Where Do Balloons Go? An Uplifting Mystery
Jamie Lee Curtis, 2000, New York: HarperCollins

The Wild Christmas Reindeer
Jan Brett, 1990, New York: Putnam and Grosset

Wordless Books

Anno's Counting Book
Mitsumasa Anno, 1986, New York: HarperTrophy

Anno's Journey
Mitsumasa Anno, 1997, New York: PaperStar

A Boy, a Dog, and a Frog
Mercer Mayer, 1992, New York: Dial Books

The Box
Kevin O'Malley, 1993, Stewart, New York: Tabori and Chang

Carl's Afternoon in the Park
Alexandra Day, 1992, New York: Farrar, Straus and Giroux

Carl's Birthday
Alexandra Day, 1997, New York: Farrar, Straus and Giroux

Carl Goes to Daycare
Alexandra Day, 1995, New York: Farrar, Straus and Giroux

Carl Goes Shopping
Alexandra Day, 1992, New York: Farrar, Straus and Giroux

Carl Makes a Scrapbook
Alexandra Day, 1994, New York: Farrar, Straus and Giroux

Carl's Masquerade
Alexandra Day, 1993, New York: Farrar, Straus and Giroux

Changes, Changes
Pat Hutchins, 1987, New York: Aladdin

Clown
Quentin Blake, 1998, New York: Holt

Creepy Castle
John Goodall, 1998, New York: McElderry

Read with Me!

Deep in the Forest
Brinton Turkle, 1992, New York: Dutton

Follow, Carl!
Alexandra Day, 1998, New York: Farrar, Straus and Giroux

FreeFall
David Weisner, 1998, New York: Morrow

Frog On His Own
Mercer Mayer, 1993, New York: Dutton

Frog, Where Are You?
Mercer Mayer, 1980, New York: Dial Books

Good Dog, Carl
Alexandra Day, 1996, New York: Simon and Schuster

Good Night, Gorilla
Peggy Rathmann, 1996, New York: Putnam

The Grey Lady and the Strawberry Snatcher
Molly Bang, 1980, New York: Simon and Schuster

Have You Seen My Duckling?
Nancy Tafuri, 1984, New York: Greenwillow

Hurricane
David Weisner, 1990, New York: Clarion Books

Midnight Adventures of Kelly, Dot, and Esmerelda
John Goodall, 1999, New York: McElderry

Mouse Around
Pat Shories, 1993, New York: Sunburst

Pancakes for Breakfast
Tomie dePaola, 1990, New York: Harvest Books

Picnic
Emily McCully, 1987, New York: HarperCollins

School
Emily McCully, 1990, New York: HarperTrophy

Sector Seven
David Weisner, 1999, Boston: Houghton Mifflin

The Snowman
Raymond Briggs, 1989, New York: Random House

Tuesday
David Weisner, 1991, New York: Clarion Books

Will's Mammoth
Rafe Martin, 1989, New York: Putnam

Read with Me!

Reader's Theatre

Another Monster at the End of This Book
Jon Stone, 1999, New York: Children's Television Workshop

Baby Beluga
Raffi, 1997, New York: Crown

Baby's Games
Judy Nayer, 1996, New York: McClanahan

City Storm
Rebel Williams, 1990, Bothell, WA: The Wright Group

Clap Your Hands
Pat Hutchins, 1992, New York: Penguin

The Doorbell Rang
Pat Hutchins, 1989, Columbus, OH: Pearson Learning

From Head to Toe
Eric Carle, 1997, New York: HarperCollins

Five Little Monkeys Jumping on the Bed
Eileen Chistelow, 1989, Boston: Houghton Mifflin

Five Little Ducks
Raffi, 1999, New York: Crown

Goldilocks and the Three Bears
Jan Brett, 1992, New York: Dodd Mead

Hand Rhymes
Marc Brown, 1993, New York: Puffin

Is Your Mama a Llama?
Deborah Guarino, 1997, New York: Scholastic

The Itsy Bitsy Spider
Iza Trapani, 1997, Watertown, MA: Charlesbridge

The Little Red Hen
Paul Galdone, 1985, Boston: Houghton Mifflin

The M & M's Counting Book
Barbara McGrath, 1994, Watertown, MA: Charlesbridge

Marsupial Sue
John Lithgow, 2001, New York: Simon and Schuster

The Monster at the End of This Book
Jon Stone, 2000, New York: Random House

The Napping House
Audrey Wood, 1984, New York: Harcourt Brace

Over the River and through the Woods
John Gurney, 1992, New York: Scholastic

Pat the Bunny
Dorothy Kunhardt, 1990, New York: Golden Books

Shake My Sillies Out
Raffi, 1990, New York: Crown

The Silly Story of Goldie Locks and the Three Squares
Grace Maccarone, 1996, New York: Cartwheel Books

Spider on the Floor
Bill Russel, 1996, New York: Crown

There Was an Old Lady Who Swallowed a Fly
Pam Adams, 1973, Swindon, England: Child's Play

The Three Little Pigs
Paul Galdone, 1994, Boston: Houghton Mifflin

The Very Busy Spider
Eric Carle, 1995, New York: Scholastic

The Very Hungry Caterpillar
Eric Carle, 1987, New York: Putnam and Grosset

We're Going on a Bear Hunt
Michael Rosen, 1997, New York: Simon and Schuster

The Wheels on the Bus
Raffi, 1998, New York: Crown

The Wide-Mouthed Frog
Kevin Faulkner, 1996, New York: Dial Books

You're Just What I Need
Ruth Krauss, 1979, New York: HarperCollins

Read with Me!

Poetry

I Saw You in the Bathtub
Alvin Schwartz, 1991, New York: HarperCollins

A Light in the Attic
Shel Silverstein, 1981, New York: HarperCollins

The New Kid on the Block
Jack Prelutsky, 1984, New York: Greenwillow

Something Big Has Been Here
Jack Prelutsky, 1990, New York: Morrow

Where the Sidewalk Ends
Shel Silverstein, 1974, New York: HarperCollins

Alphabet and Number Books

26 Letters and 99 Cents
Tara Hoban, 1987, New York: Greenwillow

A–Z
Sandra Boynton, 1995, New York: Simon and Schuster

The A–Z Beastly Jamboree
Robert Bender, 1999, New York: Puffin

Brian Wildsmith's ABC
Brian Wildsmith, 1996, New York: Starbright Books

Alphabears
Kathleen Hague, 1991, New York: Holt

Alpha Bugs: A Pop-Up Alphabet
David Carter, 1995, New York: Simon and Schuster

Alphabet City
Stephen Johnson, 1996, New York: Viking

Cock-a-Doodle-Do: A Farmyard Counting Book
Steve Lavis, 2001, New York: Ragged Bears USA

Farm Alphabet Book
Jane Miller, 1978, New York: Scholastic

How Many Bugs in a Box?
David Carter, 1988, New York: Simon and Schuster

How Many Feet? How Many Tails? A Book of Math Riddles
Marilyn Burns, 1996, New York: Scholastic

Kippers A to Z: An Alphabet Adventure
Mick Inkpen, 2001, New York: Harcourt

Learn to Count: Funny Bunnies
Cyndy Szekeres, 2000, New York: Cartwheel Books

Monster Math
Grace Maccarone, 1999, New York: Harcourt

Read with Me!

Numbears
Kathleen Hague, 1999, New York: Holt

Richard Scarry's Find Your ABC's
Richard Scarry, 1993, New York: Random House

Tricky Puppies
Judy Nayer, 1996, New York: McClanahan

Waiting for the Bus
Barry Smith, 2001, London: Tango Books

What Comes in 2's, 3's, & 4's?
Suzanne Aker, 1992, New York: Aladdin Books

Phonics/Phonological Awareness

Andy: That's My Name
Tomie DePaola, 1999, New York: Aladdin.

The Bob Book Series
Bobby Lynn Maslen, New York: Scholastic

Bob Books First! (2000)
Bob Books Fun! (2000)
Bob Books Plus! (1996)
Bob Books Wow! (2000)

The Bus for Us
Suzanne Bloom, 2001, Honesdale, PA: Boyd Mills

Fox in Socks
Dr. Suess, 1965, New York: Random House

Grandpa's Teeth
Rod Clement, 1999, New York: HarperCollins

Hop on Pop
Dr. Suess, 1963, New York: Random House

Hurray for Wodney Wat
Helen Lester, 1999, New York: Houghton Mifflin

I Heard, Said the Bird
Polly Berends, 1998, New York: Puffin Books

Mice Are Nice
Judy Nayer, 1996, New York: McClanahan

Miss Bindergarten Gets Ready for Kindergarten
Joseph Slate, 2001, New York: Puffin

Mrs. McNosh Hangs Up Her Wash
Sarah Weeks, 1998, New York: HarperCollins

Pig in a Wig
Judy Nayer, 1999, New York: Peachtree

Read with Me!

Books for Older Readers

Just for Fun
(Great Stories, Pictures, Vocabulary, and Humor)

Bartholomew and the Oobleck
Dr. Suess, 1970, New York: Random House

Chocolate Moose for Dinner
Fred Gwynne, 1988, New York: Aladdin

CinderEdna
Ellen Jackson, 1998, New York: Mulberry Books

Dear Peter Rabbit
Alma Flor Ada, 1997, New York: Aladdin

Grandpa's Teeth
Rod Clement, 1999, New York: HarperCollins

The House on East 88th Street
Bernard Waber, 1975, Boston: Houghton Mifflin

The Jolly Christmas Postman
Janet Ahlberg, 2001, New York: Little, Brown

The Jolly Postman: Or Other People's Letters
Janet Ahlberg, 2001, New York: Little, Brown

The King Who Rained
Fred Gwynne, 1988, New York: Aladdin

Leo the Late Bloomer
Robert Kraus, 1994, New York: HarperCollins

Look-Alikes
Joan Steiner, 1998, New York: Little, Brown

Miss Nelson Is Missing
Harry Allard and James Marshall, 1970, Boston: Houghton Mifflin

A Porcupine Named Fluffy
Helen Lester, 1986, Boston: Houghton Mifflin

Prince Cinders
Babette Cole, 1997, New York: Putnam

The Stinky Cheeseman and Other Fairly Stupid Tales
Jon Scieszka, 1993, New York: Viking

Tacky the Penguin
Helen Lester, 1988, Boston: Houghton Mifflin

The Three Little Wolves and the Big Bad Pig
Eugene Trivizas, 1997, New York: Aladdin

The Three Pigs
David Wiesner, 2001, New York: Clarion Books

The True Story of the Three Little Pigs
Jon Scieszka, 1996, New York: Puffin

Two Bad Ants
Chris Van Allsberg, 1998, Boston: Houghton Mifflin

Who Took My Hairy Toe?
Shuttu Crum, 2001, New York: Whitman

Wolf
Becky Bloom, 1999, New York: Grolier

Velcome
Kevin O'Malley, 1999, New York: Walker

Books for Visual Learners

The Complete Castle
Nick Denchfield and Steven Cox, 1996, London: MacMillan

Eye Popping Optical Illusions
Michael Dispezio, 2001, New York: Sterling

How Would You Survive as an Ancient Greek?
Fiona MacDonald and Mark Bergen, 1996, Danberry, CT: Watts

How Would You Survive in the Middle Ages?
Fiona MacDonald, 1997, Danberry, CT: Watts

I Spy Series
Walter Wick and Jean Marzollo, New York: Cartwheel Books

> **I Spy Christmas (1992)**
> **I Spy Extreme Challenger (2000)**
> **I Spy Funhouse (1993)**
> **I Spy Little Animals (1998)**
> **I Spy Mystery (1993)**
> **I Spy Spooky Night (1996)**

Look-Alikes
Joan Steiner, 1998, New York: Little, Brown

Marvelous Mazes
Juliet Snape, 1994, New York: Abrams

Mazes!
Susanna Gee (Ed.), 1998, New York: Dutton

A Medieval Castle: Inside Story
Fiona MacDonald and Mark Bergin, 1993, Lincolnwood, IL: Bedrick Books

Optical Illusion Magic
Michael Dispazio, 2000, New York: Sterling

Star Wars Incredible Cross Sections
David West Reynolds, 1998, New York: DK Publishing

Star Wars Incredible Cross Sections: Episode I

David West Reynolds, 1999, New York: DK Publishing

Stephen Biesty's Cross Sections Series

Stephen Biesty and Richard Platt, New York: DK Publishing

Castle: Stephen Biesty's Cross Sections (1994)

The Coolest Cross Sections Ever! (2001)

Incredible Body (1998)

Incredible Cross Sections (1992)

Incredible Everything (1997)

Incredible Explosions (1996)

Where's Waldo Series

Martin Handford, Cambridge, MA: Candlewick Press

Where's Waldo? (1997)

Where's Waldo? The Fantastic Journey (1997)

Where's Waldo? In Hollywood (1997)

Where's Waldo Now? (1997)

Where's Waldo? The Wonder Book (1997)

Comic Anthologies

Calvin and Hobbes Collections

Bill Watterson, Kansas City, MO: Andrews McMeel

The Authoritative Calvin and Hobbes (1990)

The Calvin and Hobbes Tenth Anniversary Book (1995)

The Days Are Just Packed (1993)

Homicidal Psycho Jungle Cat (1994)

It's a Magical World (1996)

Something Under the Bed Is Drooling (1999)

There's Treasure Everywhere (1996)

The Far Side Galleries

Gary Larson, Kansas City, MO: Andrews McMeel

Far Side Gallery (1984)

Far Side Gallery 2 (1986)

Far Side Gallery 3 (1988)

Far Side Gallery 4 (1993)

Far Side Gallery 5 (1995)

Garfield Series

Jim Davis, New York: Ballantine Books

Garfield Beefs Up (2000)

Garfield Feeds the Kitty (1999)

Garfield Gains Weight (1988)

Garfield: His Nine Lives (1988)

Garfield Sits Around the House (1985)

The Garfield Treasury (1982)

Give Me Coffee and No One Gets Hurt (1999)

Peanuts Series

Charles M. Schulz, New York: Ballantine Books

A Boy Named Charlie Brown (2001)

It's a Big World, Charlie Brown (2001)

It's a Dog's Life, Snoopy (2001)

Kick the Football, Charlie Brown! (2001)

Appendix B

Special Interest Books

101 Easy-to-Do Magic Tricks
Bill Tarr, 1993, Mineola, NY: Dover

Album of Horses
Marguerite Henry, 1993, New York: Aladdin Books

And the Fans Roared
Joe Garner and Bob Costas, 2000, Naperville, IL: Sourcebooks

Bats
Dee Stuart, 1994, Minneapolis, MN: First Avenue Editions

Eyewitness: Butterfly and Moth
Paul Ernest Sutton Whaley, 2000, New York: DK Publishing

Eyewitness: Shark
Miranda MacQuitty, 2000, New York: DK Publishing

Eyewitness: Whale
Vassili Papastavrou, 2000, New York: DK Publishing

The Guinness Book of Records
2002, New York: Time Home Entertainment

Insects
Robin Bernard, 2001, Washington, DC: National Geographic Society

Kid's Book of Magic Tricks
Michael Smith, 1993, Wilton, CT: Morris

Penguins
Robin Bernar, 1999, New York: Scholastic

Chapter Books

Beginning/Intermediate Chapter Books

The American Girl Collections
New York: Pleasant Company Publications

Examples from this collection include:

Changes for Addy, Bradford Brown, 1994

Felicity's Surprise, Valerie Tripp, 1991

Happy Birthday, Molly! Valerie Tripp, 1987

Josephina Saves the Day, Valerie Tripp, 1998

Meet Kirsten, Janet Beeler Shaw, 1986

Meet Samantha, Susan Adler, 1991

Arthur Chapter Book Series
Marc Brown, New York: Little, Brown

Examples from this series include:

Arthur Meets a President (1992)

Arthur Writes a Story (1998)

Arthur's Baby (1990)

Arthur's Chicken Pox (1996)

Arthur's First Sleepover (1996)

Arthur's Tooth (1987)

Arthur's TV Trouble (1997)

Babe the Gallant Pig
Dick King-Smith, 1993, New York: Random House

The Best Christmas Pageant Ever
Barbara Robinson, 1988, New York: HarperTrophy

The BFG
Roald Dahl, 1998, New York: Puffin Books

The Bunny Hop
Teddy Slater, 1992, New York: Scholastic

The Captain Underpants Series

Dav Pilkey, New York: Blue Sky Press

Examples from this series include:

Captain Underpants and the Attack of the Talking Toilet (1999)

Captain Underpants and the Extra Crunchy Book O' Fun (2001)

Captain Underpants and the Plot of Professor Poopypants (2000)

Captain Underpants and the Wrath of the Wicked Wedgie Woman (2001)

Charlie and the Chocolate Factory

Roald Dahl, 1998, New York: Puffin Books

Charlotte's Web

E.B. White, 1999, New York: HarperTrophy

The Dear America Series

New York: Scholastic

Examples from this series include:

I Thought My Soul Would Rise and Fly, Joyce Hansen, 1997

A Journey to a New World, Kathryn Lasky, 1996

The Winter of the Red Snow, Kristiana Gregory, 1996

Hank the Cowdog Series

John Erickson, New York: Puffin Books

The Case of the One-Eyed Killer Studhorse (1999)

The Case of the Vampire Cat (1999)

The Curse of the Incredible Priceless Corncob (1999)

Faded Love (1999)

The Further Adventures of Hank the Cowdog (1999)

The Original Adventures of Hank the Cowdog (1999)

The Wounded Buzzard on Christmas Eve (1999)

James and the Giant Peach

Roald Dahl, 2000, New York: Penguin

Jeremy Thatcher, Dragon Hatcher

Bruce Coville, 1992, New York: Minstrel Books

Read with Me!

The Kid Next Door and Other Headaches
Janice Lee Smith, 1987, New York: HarperCollins

The Magic Tree House Series
Mary Pope Osborn, New York: Random House

Dinosaurs Before Dark (1992)

The Knight at Dawn (1993)

Mummies in the Morning (1993)

Pirates Past Noon (1994)

The Phantom Tollbooth
Norton Juster, 1993, New York: Foresman

Mr. Popper's Penguins
Richard and Florence Atwater, 1994, New York: Scholastic

The Chronicles of Narnia
C.S. Lewis, New York: HarperCollins

The Horse and His Boy (1954)

The Last Battle (1956)

The Lion, the Witch, and the Wardrobe (1950)

The Magician's Nephew (1955)

Prince Caspian (1951)

The Silver Chair (1953)

The Voyage of the Dawn Treader (1952)

Rabbit Hill
Robert Lawson, 1994, New York: Viking Press

Rats on the Roof and Other Stories
James Marshall, 1997, New York: Puffin

Ramona the Pest
Beverly Cleary, 1996, New York: Foresman

The Stepping Stone Series

Ann Camerion, New York: Random House

Julian, Dream Doctor (1990)

Julian's Glorious Summer (1987)

More Stories Huey Tells (1997)

More Stories Julian Tells (1989)

The Stories Huey Tells (1997)

The Stories Julian Tells (1989)

The Witches

James Roald, 1998, New York: Puffin Books

A Wrinkle in Time

Madeleine L'Engle, 1973, New York: Yearling Books

Advanced Chapter Books

All Creatures Great and Small
James Herriot, 1981, New York: Bantam

Brighty of the Grand Canyon
Marguerite Henry, 1991, New York: Aladdin

Harry Potter Series
J.K. Rawling, New York: Scholastic

Harry Potter and the Chamber of Secrets (2000)

Harry Potter and the Goblet of Fire (2000)

Harry Potter and the Prisoner of Azkaban (2001)

Harry Potter and the Sorcerer's Stone (1999)

The Hobbit: Or There and Back Again
J.R.R. Tolkien, 1999, Boston: Houghton Mifflin

The Chronicles of Prydain
Lloyd Alexander, New York: Yearling Books

The Black Cauldron (1999)

The Book of Three (1999)

The Castle of Llyr (1999)

The High King (1999)

Taran Wanderer (1969)

Watership Down
Richard Adams, 1989, New York: Avon Books

Appendix C

PURCHASING INFORMATION

The books suggested in the lists in Appendix B can be purchased from a number of sources. Most can be ordered through local bookstores (e.g., Barnes & Noble or Walden Books) or various online book sellers (e.g., *Amazon.com* or *Borders.com*). Some favorite vendors are listed below (in alphabetical order).

The Bookmen, Inc.
525 North Third Street
Minneapolis, MN 55401

This company carries many of the take-home books for the *Read with Me!* School program and many alternate titles.

Lakeshore Learning Materials
P.O. Box 6261
2695 E. Dominguez Street
Carson, CA 90749
1-800-421-5354
www.LakehoreLearning.com

You can get fairly inexpensive book bags filled with props to support many reader's theatre activities from this vendor.

Scholastic
P.O. Box 7502
2931 E. McCarty Street
Jefferson City, MO 65101
1-800-724-6527
www.Scholastic.com

Scholastic publishes an early childhood catalog, a Big Books catalog, and a supplementary materials catalog that has many of the titles on the book lists as well as supplementary materials such as book bags and Big Book stands. They also provide a 30% discount to educators.

The Wright Group
19201 120th Avenue NE, Suite 100
Bothell, WA 98011-9512
www.WrightGroup.com

The Wright group carries a large selection of Big Books.

Appendix D

OVERHEAD PRESENTATION

Optional Narrative

The following narrative corresponds to the color PowerPoint program found on the accompanying CD-ROM. If you do not wish to use the PowerPoint presentation, you can print all slides (in black and white or color) and use them as handouts or overheads. If you use the overheads, you will want to take along a marker for certain slides (as noted in the narrative that follows). If you are using the PowerPoint presentation, the information is revealed with each mouse click. In the text that follows, each [*] represents a click of the mouse. Regardless of the format you choose, you will want to run through the program several times to familiarize yourself with both the material and the timing.

You may pick and choose the slides you wish to use depending on your audience. You will need to slightly modify your delivery for parents versus educators, but both groups will benefit from this short overview regarding language and literacy and the importance of joint reading interactions during the preschool years and beyond.

Overhead 1—Title

*Overhead 2—Language and Literacy Grow Together

There is a strong link between [*] oral language and [*] written language. In fact, some people argue that once written language is decoded, reading and talking are the same thing! For children to learn to talk, they need to be talked to. For them to learn to read, they need to be talked to and read to! As one area grows stronger, it helps the other grow stronger as well.

Appendix D

*Overhead 3—Oral Communication Is the Key to Classroom Success

Click to reveal each point on the slide. Then say:

The next slide will help you understand why talking and listening are so important to reading, writing, and learning in school.

*Overhead 4—Language/Literacy Hierarchy

This is an extremely powerful slide if used correctly. If you are using overheads, you will need to have a dry erase marker available. Alternatively, the PowerPoint program included on the accompanying CD-ROM will complete the graphic for you. The best way to demonstrate the importance of oral language to reading and writing, and ultimately all school subjects, is to demonstrate it using the Language/Literacy Hierarchy.

Read with Me!

At the base of this pyramid is receptive oral language, or listening. This is the foundation of all learning, it is the first area to develop, and it is the largest area of development. Think about how babies learn to talk. They can understand what you tell them long before they can say the words. For instance, a 10-month-old baby turns to look for Daddy when someone says "Daddy." Adults also have a much larger listening vocabulary—that is, words they can understand—than their speaking vocabulary. For example, you could probably understand parts of a lecture on brain surgery, but you probably are not ready to go and give a lecture on the same topic!

The next level is expressive oral language, or talking. This area is slightly smaller than listening since you understand many more words than you actually use in your spoken vocabulary. Obviously, you do not use words in oral communication that are not within your scope of comprehension—that is, part of your receptive vocabulary—although you may know people you suspect of doing this! But for most of us, the size of our expressive language vocabulary is directly dependent on the size of our receptive language vocabulary. The same is true for children.

The next level is your receptive written language, or reading. Now, you might be able to sound out a word like this: [Write on board, slide, or overhead] Spasmophonia. *How do you pronounce this word? What does it mean?* [Audience members generally say they do not know what it means] *Then, would you say that you read the word? What if a child had no idea what an owl was. Even if he or she could sound out the word, would that be reading? No, of course not. In order to truly read a word, not just sound out a bunch of letters, you must be able to comprehend its meaning. So, your reading vocabulary is directly dependent on the size of your oral language base. In case you were wondering,* **spasmophonia** *means "inability to speak due to a spasm of the larynx."*

The fourth level, expressive written language, which is, of course, writing, is directly dependent on the size of your reading vocabulary. In the same way as with oral language, you do not write words you cannot read. Consequently, your writing abilities are limited by your reading abilities.

On the very top are all the other academic areas that require oral and written skills in order to be proficient. These include math, social studies, English, science, and even physical education!

Now, as interesting as all this is, it is not the most impressive thing about this slide! Let's say that a child enters school with a slightly smaller than average receptive vocabulary. This could be for any reason. Maybe he or she has not had a chance to visit a farm or a zoo or a grocery store. Maybe there is an underlying problem with language development. Maybe he *or she was not read to. Whatever the reason, this would mean that the child's receptive oral language base is going to be reduced.* [Click to reveal a line, or if you are using overheads, draw a line with a dry erase marker to slightly decrease the size of the bottom tier, like the sketch below] *That means that the child's expressive oral language is also going to be somewhat smaller* [Click to reveal a line, or or draw a line across the next tier]—*which means his or her reading potential is also decreased* [Click to reveal a line, or or draw a line across the next tier]. *This decreases the size of the writing base* [Click to reveal a line, or or draw a line across the next tier], *and when you see what has happened to the size of the top tier* [Click to reveal a line, or draw a line across the next tier], *you no longer wonder why so many children are having trouble in math and science!*

Language/Literacy Hierarchy

CONTENT AREAS
WRITING
(Receptive WRITTEN Language)
READING
(Receptive WRITTEN Language)
TALKING
(Expressive ORAL Language)
LISTENING
(Receptive ORAL Language)

Hopefully, this demonstration gives you a graphic understanding of the importance of helping children build a language base that is as broad as possible. The strategies and techniques that you will be learning during these workshops will help you do exactly that!

Overhead 5—Read with Me! Core Beliefs

The Read with Me! *program is based on several core beliefs about reading with children.*

Read with Me!

*Overhead 6

Even if children are taught every phonics skill in the book, they will not want to read if reading is not a pleasant experience!

*Overhead 7 and *Overhead 8

Click to reveal each slide. You could add:

We cannot stress enough the value of what parents can do to help get their children off to a good start in school. We need you!

Appendix D

*Overhead 9

You could add:

What you do at home can make a substantial impact on your child's eventual success in school. But this does not mean workbooks and drill! It means helping children learn to enjoy reading while you are building language and early reading skills together.

*Overhead 10—Stages of Reading

Steve Bialostok, in his book Raising Readers, *suggested that there are nine steps, or stages, to becoming an independent reader.*

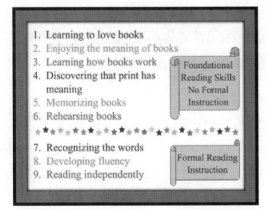

*Overhead 11

These stages are [Click to reveal each stage]

Most people think that children go to school to learn to read. [Click to complete the slide graphics before continuing] *However, notice that it is only the last three stages that are part of what we consider formal reading instruction. That is, what children learn about reading when they go to school to learn to read. Many teachers assume that children have already attained the skills of the first six stages*

Read with Me!

before children even walk into school the first day. Now, how do you think children learn these things? By engaging in reading experiences! Just as children learn to talk by talking, they learn about reading by reading. Children who do not have these skills are at a distinctive disadvantage when they enter their formal schooling years.

*Overhead 12—*Read with Me!* Strategies

Over the course of these three sessions [or whatever you have decided to provide], *we will be teaching you about six different strategies and types of books that you can use to help children build the language and prereading skills that are so vital to their eventual success at school and in everyday life. We have found that these strategies help children enjoy reading while they are learning to read. These six strategies are* [Click to reveal each strategy]

*Overhead 13—Reading with Children Should Be…

Appendix D

*Overhead 14—Fun!

Click four times to reveal all sunbursts.

*Overhead 15—Stress Free

Click two times to reveal the rest of the graphic.

*Overhead 16

You could add:

Now, let's get reading and have some fun!

FREQUENTLY ASKED QUESTIONS

Frequently Asked Questions Regarding Development and Implementation

1. Who should teach the workshops?

We suggest that the program coordinator be a certified educator with expertise in the areas of language and literacy. However, facilitators can be anyone who has a strong interest in working with young children and has a good working knowledge of, or experience with, the *Read with Me!* strategies.

2. How do I get parents to participate?

It helps if you invite parents personally. Try to schedule the workshops at times that are convenient for parents, such as evenings or even weekends. You may wish to provide incentives, such as free books and materials, babysitting, and, if possible, transportation. Your best advertising is word of mouth, so do not be discouraged if your first group is small. Word gets around when the experience is positive. It also helps if you share what you are doing with classroom teachers. They often welcome the support.

If you are working with the children directly, try to involve parents by video-taping sessions, sending home books, and having the children read to their parents to show off newly learned skills. Make sure parents have plenty of information about the goals of the program. We do not want reading at home to become stressful!

3. When is the best time of day to schedule workshops?

Some parents are available during school hours, but most prefer early evening times. It is a good idea to survey parents to find out their preferred meeting times. Then, do your best to schedule the workshops according to parent preferences.

4. Do I have to serve food?

No, food is definitely an optional component to the *Read with Me!* programs. However, it is a really nice way to make participants feel like they are welcome to stay and browse through books on display. Also, any children who come with their parents (but were in the child-care area) can join the group for a snack and look at the books along with their parents.

If you are feeling very creative, you can provide a snack that ties into one of the stories. For instance, you can serve muffins in honor of *If You Give a Moose a Muffin* or bananas for *Goodnight Gorilla*. We have even had parents volunteer to bring refreshments for later sessions.

5. How do I get parents to share their home reading experiences?

Initially, we find it works well if the facilitators are willing to share their own experiences regarding reading with children (either with their own children or with students with whom they have worked). In addition, if you have done your job right, by the time parents come back for the second workshop, they are bursting with stories they cannot wait to share.

6. May I list *Read with Me!* on a child's IEP?

Most IEPs do not require that specific methods for achieving goals and objectives be listed on the document. However, if your district does require this, you are free to use the name and the reference.

Frequently Asked Questions from Workshop Participants

1. How old should my child be before I start reading to him or her?

It is never too early to start reading with your child. The bond that develops between parents and babies begins at birth. (Some researchers suggest this begins to develop even before birth). Reading and talking with babies strengthens this bond that is so critical to all future social interactions (including learning). Babies and infants are responding mostly to your voice—the tone, the inflection, and the familiarity. Later on, toddlers learn to enjoy the rhythm of reading and will start to look at interesting pictures. Even more importantly, they are learning that reading is a special thing that you do with people who love you. This is when you begin to plant the desire to read in your child.

2. When is my child too old to be read to?

This is the flip side of the previous question. It has a similar answer. Your children are never too old to be read to. There are many advantages to reading with older children—for both you and your child! For instance, since children can understand much more than they can read, your reading together times can help children experience literature that is too advanced for them to read, but not for them to understand and enjoy! Also, the need for parent-child "together time" does not end just because your child has gotten older. In fact, in many ways, it is even more important for older children to have some individual time with a parent—especially if there are younger children in the household.

3. What if I make mistakes when I read?

Your child is not listening for mistakes. He or she is enjoying the story, the talking, and the experience of reading together. Don't be afraid to make mistakes! It helps your child see that even adults sometimes have trouble reading too.

4. What if I don't have time to read every day?

It is often difficult to read every day, and some days it is nearly impossible. However, you do not have to spend hours and hours reading with your child to make the reading interaction meaningful. It is important, however, to find time to read with your child on a regular basis. Try starting the bedtime routine 10 minutes earlier. Let your child stay up 10 minutes later. Don't worry about the dishes in the sink or the dust fluffies under the bed. Children grow up quickly. The cobwebs in the corner, on the other hand, will still be there when children are grown. Try to think of reading together as an investment in your child's future.

5. My child doesn't like it when I ask "friendly" questions. Do I ask them anyway?

Some children love the "friendly" format and are relieved that "scary" questions are not being asked anymore. However, some children indicate that they do not like the new questions you are asking. Usually this is because your child is not used to you asking these kinds of questions. Some children find the scary questions easy to answer—especially if they have read the book with you many times. They know the questions you typically ask, and they are ready with the answer. While this isn't a bad thing, it does not encourage them to think critically about the story or encourage them to use more complex language. Gradually add friendly questions into your shared reading times to encourage your child to develop these important skills.

6. What if my child wants to read the same book over and over and over?

This is a very normal, and very positive, reading behavior of young readers. Children love to revisit favorite characters and stories that they can recite with you through paired reading—or maybe by "reading" the entire book themselves! Some children are adamant that you read certain parts of the book in exactly the same way or read exactly the same books in exactly the same order. This can get a bit exasperating for a parent who is ready to try something new! Take turns picking books so that your child is introduced to some new characters and stories. But, do not be surprised when the old favorites are still requested over and over again.

7. My child's other parent does not live with us. How can I get him or her involved with using these reading strategies?

You may want to consider designating a special "book bag" that your child can use to take his or her favorite books along on visits to the other parent's home. Talk to your child about sharing the new books with "Daddy" or "Mommy." The enthusiasm your child demonstrates while reading his or her favorite books can be infectious. You may want to include copies of the handouts from the workshops and videotapes (if your child is in the *Read with Me!* School program).

8. What if my child doesn't like a particular book?

Don't feel that your child has to like a particular book just because you or someone else happens to like it. There are many, many books to choose from that support *Read with Me!* strategies. If your child doesn't like a book, put it away and choose another. Try it again some other time and see what happens!

9. How do I model reading for my children when they won't let me sit and read a book?

Do not be afraid to tell your child that it is your turn to read and you must not be disturbed. Then, sit the child down next to you, hand him or her a book, set the timer and both of you can "read" at the same time. Your child may choose to get up and do something else (which is fine), but he or she may not interrupt you while you are reading. Initially, set the timer for a very short amount of time—perhaps one minute. You can gradually increase the amount of time to an appropriate interval. Eventually, your child will begin to see that reading is an important adult activity. Since children like to copy adult behaviors, do not be surprised to see him or her pick up the newspaper and "read" along with you!

10. I wonder if protective services knows about *Good Dog, Carl?*

We just had to slip this one in because we almost always have someone voice this sentiment in one form or another every time we share this funny, wonderful story. Carl is a large dog who is frequently left in charge of a young child with no adult present.

11. My child is visually impaired. How can I make reading better for him or her?

You can adapt all the *Read with Me!* strategies for a child who is visually impaired. Echo reading helps a child learn the story so that eventually he or she can participate in paired reading. Take time to describe the pictures and what is happening in them. Use rich vocabulary to help your child visualize the illustrations. Do not be afraid to ask "friendly" questions and encourage your child to predict what might come next. He or she can also benefit from reader's theatre activities in the same ways as children whose visual acuity is more typical. All these strategies can help your child become more engaged in the reading interaction to build those important language and early literacy skills.

12. My child's attention span is really short. What do I do?

Select books that have bright pictures, lots of rhythm and rhyme, and very few words on each page. Do not try to read books that are too long or too wordy. Helping your child become engaged in the reading through echo reading, paired reading, reader's theatre, or any of the other *Read with Me!* strategies can also help get, and keep, your child's interest. Keeping the reading session short, using lots of expression in your voice, and allowing your child to select and hold the book can also assist in making reading together more fun for both of you.

13. Isn't my child just memorizing the books—not really reading them?

We hope that is exactly what your child is doing! An earlier step in the reading process than actually reading the words is memorizing books. As children learn to recite books orally, they begin to realize that what is coming out of their mouths is represented by the squiggles on the page. This helps them understand that what they say can be written down and read back. Before long, they actually will be reading the words!

14. Does *Read with Me!* work with at-risk groups?

Children from other groups that may be at risk for delayed or impoverished language and literacy skills—such as those from homes with lower socioeconomic status (SES) levels and from homes where English is not spoken as a first language—can also benefit from the strategies and techniques associated with *the Read with Me!* program. Even parents who are not literate can use many of the *Read with Me!* strategies to help their children build skills vital to reading and talking. In addition, guidance in the selection of children's literature that facilitates language and literacy development is especially valuable for those who are on a limited budget or those who are unfamiliar with the culture.

15. Can I come back next year?

Absolutely! How about as a facilitator? Bring a friend!

REFERENCES

Adams, M. (1990). *Beginning to read: Thinking and learning about print.* Cambridge, MA: MIT Press.

Bialostok, S. (1992). *Raising readers: Helping your child to literacy.* Winnipeg: Peguis Books.

Bishop, D.V.M., and Adams, C. (1990). A prospective study of the relationship between specific language impairment, phonological disorders, and reading retardation. *Journal of Child Psychology and Psychiatry, 31,* 102–105.

Blachman, B. (1994). Early literacy acquisition: The role of phonological awareness. In G. Wallach and K. Butler (Eds.), *Language learning disabilities in school-age children and adolescents* (pp. 253–274). New York: Macmillan.

Bricker, D. (1986). *Early education of at-risk and handicapped infants, toddlers, and preschool children.* Glenview, IL: Foresman.

Bruner, J. (1983). Child talk. Learning how to use temperament, and the risk of childhood behavioral problems: I. Relationship between parental characteristics and changes in children's temperament over time. *American Journal of Orthopsychiatry, 47,* 568–576.

Catts, H. (1993). The relationship between speech-language impairments and reading disabilities. *Journal of Speech and Hearing Research, 36,* 948–958.

Crowe, L.K., Norris, J.A., and Hoffman, P.R. (2000). Facilitating storybook interactions between mothers and their preschoolers with language impairment. *Communication Disorders Quarterly, 21,* 131–146.

Davig, D., and Jacobson, C. (1998). *Reading together in kindergarten handbook.* Holmen, WI: Holmen School District.

Ellis Weismer, S. (1996). Morphological learning by children with language impairments. *Topics in Language Disorders, 17*(1), 33–44.

Fey, M. (1986). *Language intervention with young children.* Newton, MA: Allyn and Bacon.

Fey, M., Catts, H., and Larrivee, L. (1995). Preparing preschoolers for the academic and social challenges of school. In M. Fey, J. Windsor, and S. Warren (Eds.), *Language intervention: Preschool through the elementary years* (pp. 3–39). Baltimore: Brookes.

Institute of Child Health and Human Development. (2002). *Report of the the National Reading Panel. Teaching children to read: An evidence-based assessment of the scientific research literature on reading and its implications for reading instruction* (NIH Publication No. 00-4769). Washington, DC: U.S. Government Printing Office.

Read with Me!

Kahmi, A., and Catts, H. (1986). Toward an understanding of developmental language and reading disorders. *Journal of Speech and Hearing Disorders, 51,* 337–347.

Magnusson, E., and Naucler, K. (1990). Reading and spelling in language disordered children—linguistic and metalinguistic prerequisites: Report on a longitudinal study. *Clinical Linguistics and Phonetics, 4,* 49–61.

Muir, N., McCaig, S., Gerylo, K., Gompf, M., Burke, T., and Lumsden, P. (2000). *Talk! Talk! Talk! Tools to facilitate language.* Eau Claire, WI: Thinking Publications.

Robertson, S., Smith, D., and Sollenberger, M. (2001, November). *The effects of parental training on the language and literacy behaviors of children.* Poster session presented at the national convention of the American Speech-Language-Hearing Association, New Orleans, LA.

Shatz, M. (1983). Communication. In P.H. Mussen (Ed.), *Handbook of child psychology: Vol. 3. Cognitive development.* New York: Wiley.

Silva, P.A., Williams, S., and McGee, R. (1985). A longitudinal study of children with developmental language delay at age three: Later intelligence, reading, and behavior problems. *Developmental Medicine and Child Neurology, 29,* 630-640.

Snow, C.E., Burns, M.S., and Griffin, P. (Eds.); Committee on Prevention of Reading Difficulties in Young Children, National Research Council. (1998). *Preventing reading difficulties in young children.* Washington, DC: National Academy Press.

Stark, R., Bernstein, L., Condino, R., Bender, M., Tallal, P., and Catts, H. (1984). Four year follow-up study of language impaired children. *Annals of Dyslexia, 34,* 44–68.

Trelease, J. (1989). *The new read-aloud handbook.* New York: Penguin.

U.S. Department of Education. (2000). *Teaching children to read.* Retrieved March 22, 2002, from http://www.nationalreadingpanel.org/Publications/publications.htm

Vygotsky, L. (1978). *Mind in society.* Cambridge: MIT Press.

Yoder, P., and Warren, S. (1993). Can prelinguistic intervention enhance the language development of children with developmental delays? In A. Kaiser and D.B. Gray (Eds.), *Enhancing children's communication: Research foundations for early language intervention* (pp. 35–63). Baltimore: Brookes.